Nonproliferation Primer

Nonproliferation Primer
Preventing the Spread of Nuclear, Chemical, and Biological Weapons

Randall Forsberg

William Driscoll

Gregory Webb

Jonathan Dean

The MIT Press
Cambridge, Massachusetts
London, England

Second printing, 1999

Copyright © by the Institute for Defense and Disarmament Studies
675 Massachusetts Avenue
Cambridge, Massachusetts 02139
617/354-4337

Printed in the United States of America.

Distributed by The MIT Press, Cambridge, Massachusetts, and London, England.

Library of Congress Cataloging-in-Publication Data

Nonproliferation primer: preventing the spread of nuclear, chemical, and
   biological weapons / Randall Forsberg . . . [et al.].
     p.   cm.
   Includes bibliographical references and index.
   ISBN 0-262-06183-X (hc: acid-free).—ISBN 0-262-56095-X (pb: acid-free)
   1. Nuclear nonproliferation. 2. Biological arms control. 3. Chemical arms
control. I. Forsberg, Randall.
JX1974.73.N68   1995
327.1'74—dc20
                                                                      95-11840
                                                                          CIP

Book designed by Miriam Avins

10 9 8 7 6 5 4 3 2

Printed in the United States of America

Contents

Tables and Figures

Acknowledgments

Large portions of this book have been excerpted from three reports on the problem of the proliferation of weapons of mass destruction published by the Office of Technology Assessment (OTA) of the United States Congress: *Proliferation of Weapons of Mass Destruction: Assessing the Risks* (August 1993); *Technologies Underlying Weapons of Mass Destruction* (December 1993); and *Export Controls and Nonproliferation Policy* (May 1994).

The OTA reports were produced by a project team supervised by Dr. Gerald L. Epstein and comprised of Dr. Dan Fenstermacher, Dr. Jonathan B. Tucker, and Dr. Thomas H. Karas, with review from an expert advisory panel that included one of this volume's authors (Randall Forsberg). The OTA reports have done a special service to the public in the United States and throughout the world, in carefully sifting, compiling, and synthesizing a tremendous amount of technical information. One purpose of this primer, which presents key points from the reports, is to make more information on this important topic available to the general public.

The authors are deeply indebted to those who prepared the original OTA reports for their fine work. In addition, we are especially grateful to Dr. Epstein, who generously provided the text of the OTA reports on disk, so as to facilitate the process of excerpting and help ensure its accuracy.

The OTA welcomes and encourages widespread dissemination and utilization of its work (which is unclassified, supported by taxpayer funds, and not copyrighted). However, it does not take responsibility for the selection or accuracy of the material presented in this volume, which has been excerpted, edited, and rearranged by the authors. Nor is OTA responsible for those portions of this book that represent entirely new material, or updates and additions to information published by OTA.

Chapters 1 and 7 of this volume, which were prepared by Randall Forsberg and Jonathan Dean, are entirely original and are not linked to OTA publications.

Chapters 2, 3, 4, 5, and 6 are made up of excerpts from the OTA reports, prepared by William Driscoll, with the following changes: cosmetic editorial changes made for reasons of style; updates on matters of proliferation and proliferation control that have occurred since the OTA reports were finalized, prepared by Gregory Webb, editor of the *Arms Control Reporter*, a monthly reference journal; and a small amount of material from other sources, which are cited in footnotes.

In the interest of brevity, much of the content of the original OTA reports could not be reproduced here. For elaboration of the material presented in Chapters 2 through 6, the interested reader is referred to the original OTA reports.

William Driscoll originally proposed this book. Frank von Hippel provided invaluable advice at an early stage. Lisbeth Gronlund and David Wright provided helpful comments on the manuscript.

The authors are grateful to Miriam Avins for a fine job of editing and book design, and to MIT Press acquisitions editor Larry Cohen for helping to make this book possible.

Chapter 1

Nonproliferation:
What One Person Can Do

The end of the Cold War has reduced the risks of an all-out nuclear war between East and West, but increased concern about the proliferation of weapons of mass destruction. The good news is that the risks of a global nuclear holocaust have plummeted. The United States and Russia have eliminated the nuclear tripwire: they have withdrawn the short-range "tactical" nuclear weapons that once marked the front lines of East-West confrontation. They have abandoned strategies of "nuclear warfighting" (aiming nuclear weapons at the opponent's forces) as a way to deter conventional war. And they have agreed to make deep cuts in their arsenals of long-range "strategic" nuclear arms. These positive changes have created a breathing space, an opportunity to address the risks posed by the global spread of nuclear, chemical, and biological weapons and of missiles and aircraft to deliver them.

The bad news is that with the collapse of the former Soviet Union, worries about proliferation have grown. Outside Russia, three other former Soviet republics now have strategic nuclear weapons on their territory. In those republics and in Russia, fissile materials or entire weapons could be stolen. Unemployed nuclear weapon scientists living at the poverty level anywhere in the former Soviet Union could emigrate to countries that can pay them a good wage for building nuclear weapons; and chemical and biological weapon facilities inherited by former Soviet republics other than Russia could be re-opened.

These are not the only worries. Long-standing conflicts in South Asia, the Middle East, and East Asia motivate ongoing efforts for countries to acquire nuclear weapons. For over 20 years, India and China have had overt nuclear capabilities, and Israel has had a covert program. Now serious efforts to acquire nuclear weapons have been exposed in Iraq and North Korea, and Pakistan may be able to assemble a bomb at short notice. Other countries, such as Iran, may follow.

What dangers does proliferation pose? In the short term, the great dangers are regional nuclear war, which could obliterate cities, kill millions, and devastate downwind areas; and nuclear terrorism—a few bombs smuggled into major cities anywhere in the world—which could wreak equal havoc. Over the longer term, there will be new nuclear threats as more and more nations acquire more sophisticated delivery systems, including short-range, intermediate-range, and intercontinental missiles, as well as advanced aircraft.

This book provides a concise overview of nonproliferation issues. It looks at the means by which countries might acquire weapons of mass destruction, the range of potential strategies to stem proliferation, current nonproliferation efforts and prospects, and possible new efforts. It covers the gamut of proliferation-related material, providing all the information citizens need to interpret, assess, and respond to ongoing developments. The primer aims to help newly concerned readers get up to speed quickly, provide a handy reference source, and give an up-to-date survey of trends, issues, and options.

Nonproliferation: Do Individual Actions Make a Difference?

For most people, issues like the global spread of nuclear weapons are important but remote, unconnected to their daily lives. The common view is, "How could I have an impact on what is going to happen in Iraq, North Korea, or Pakistan or even in countries more open to dialogue, such as India or Israel?"

Obviously, citizens of any country can influence the nuclear policies of their own nation far more readily than they can affect the policies of nations in distant regions. Nevertheless, there are many ways, both direct and indirect, in which what happens in the United States and other industrial nations can affect the prospects for proliferation of weapons of mass destruction in the Third World.

In considering how the average person might have some impact on the course of events, it is helpful to think of the world as comprising concentric and overlapping circles of community. At home, these circles generally involve family, town (or part of a city), state or region, and then nation. Abroad, the United States coordinates its policies with other Western nations, particularly Canada, West European countries, and Japan. In addition, on a number of relevant issues, the United States has negotiated common or mutually acceptable positions with Russia and China, and, in a different sense, with allied or friendly Third World countries, such as South Korea, Taiwan, Israel, and Egypt.

Individuals in each of these "communities" are susceptible to changes of mind and heart brought about by information, informed debate, or lobbying. Still, the reader might respond, these expanding circles of community, at least for a typical US citizen, do not extend to the countries most likely to be the next to acquire nuclear, chemical, or biological weapons.

The nations that are the leading candidates for proliferation can, however, be directly influenced by a combination of pressures brought to bear by other nations. Carrots and sticks—incentives and sanctions—that can play a decisive role are discussed in detail in Chapter 5. In some cases, sufficiently powerful positive incentives may induce a country to halt its nuclear weapon program. One current example involves US efforts to persuade North Korea to shut down its program in exchange for diplomatic recognition, modern nuclear reactors, trade, and economic aid. In other cases the world might lean more heavily on the stick: this applies, for example, to the UN Security Council–sponsored steps, taken under the threat of military sanctions, to identify, dismantle, and monitor the shut-down of Iraq's facilities for building nuclear, chemical, and biological weapons and short-range ballistic missiles. To prevent proliferation in countries with little advanced industrial infrastructure, export controls offer a way for more advanced nations to obstruct and delay the acquisition of nuclear weapons and long-range missiles for decades. And last but not least, the growth and expression of public opinion condemning the acquisition and use of weapons of mass destruction can lead to self-restraint. This is exemplified by the case of India, which developed the materials and know-how to make nuclear explosives, but once it had conducted a successful nuclear test, took no overt steps to build a nuclear weapon arsenal.

The strength of direct measures by the international community to stop proliferation—incentives, sanctions, export controls, and public condemnation—will vary with the vigor of the efforts and the extent of the international consensus behind them. This is where involvement by individuals throughout the industrial world—and perhaps, if they can be reached by independent mass media, individuals throughout the developing world—can make a difference. If there is strong, visible public support for effective, high-priority nonproliferation efforts, then governments are likely to work much harder on this issue than if the public seems indifferent.

Still, some readers might object, US and other government officials are undoubtedly motivated to try to prevent proliferation, and they have ready access to expert advisers and classified intelligence. Why should ordinary citizens undertake to seek out information, build public concern, and reach public officials merely to reinforce a concern that public officials already have?

Public awareness and support matter because export controls, trade and aid inducements, and armed enforcement and monitoring all cost money. Not big money compared with, say, the funding of the US Defense Department, but enough to attract some attention in the increasingly fierce budget battles in all industrial nations. Public concern and support help ensure that government officials hold firm on proliferation policy despite the short-term costs, giving the issue top priority when other foreign and military policy goals compete for attention, action, or funding.

Equally important, citizen involvement is essential for the development of a new approach to security among the major military powers—an approach that, along with the carrots and sticks, might help stop the further spread of weapons of mass destruction. For the past quarter of a century, since the nuclear Nonproliferation Treaty (NPT) entered into force in 1970, the world's leading military powers have tried to stop others from acquiring nuclear weapons while still relying heavily on nuclear deterrence in their own policies. In effect, the major powers have said, "Do as we say, not as we do." Not surprisingly, this attitude has met with resentment and rebuff on the part of many Third World nations.

There are many changes the five acknowledged nuclear weapon powers could make in their own security policies to strengthen nonproliferation efforts. Some changes concern policies that relate directly to nuclear weapons and fissile material. For example, experts have long argued that to establish a strong nonproliferation regime, the nuclear powers should stop all testing of nuclear weapons. In 1963, the United States, the Soviet Union, and the United Kingdom agreed to ban nuclear tests above ground (and in outer space and under water) for environmental and health reasons, but to permit continued explosions of nuclear weapons underground. Public interest groups point out that it is hypocritical and signals a lack of good faith for the nuclear powers to keep developing and testing nuclear weapons while telling other nations not to acquire such weapons. Other nuclear-related measures that would strengthen nonproliferation efforts include agreements by the nuclear powers to stop producing fissile material for weapons, to accept international inspections of nuclear power plants, comparable to those required of non-nuclear weapon states under the NPT, and to make deep cuts in their nuclear arsenals.

Other measures to help stem proliferation involve steps to reduce fears of global or regional conventional (non-nuclear) war. All nuclear threshold and near-nuclear states are engaged in long-standing regional conflicts with neighboring countries; nearly all have very large arsenals of sophisticated conventional weaponry (combat aircraft, tanks, heavy artillery, and so on); and all have engaged in at least one large-scale conventional war with a major regional opponent since 1945. There is, thus, a very strong relationship between the expectation or fear of a major conventional war and interest in acquiring nuclear weapons, which could serve either to deter conventional attack by a regional adversary or to deter intervention in a regional war by one of the nuclear weapon states.

Ultimately, the most enduring and stable resolution of regional conflicts will come from the resolution of the political issues that underlie such conflicts, or the creation of participatory secular governments, or both. For the near term, however, fears and risks of major conventional war can be greatly alleviated through security guarantees and through arms control and confidence-building measures of both global and regional types. A reduction in the threat of major conventional war would, in turn, facilitate progress on the basic political issues.

The end of the Cold War has created an unprecedented opportunity for the world's major military powers—which are also the main nuclear weapon states and the world's sole producers and exporters of technologically advanced conventional weapon systems—to cooperate in fostering the development of global and regional security regimes that will minimize the risks of major conventional war and build confidence in the peace. As yet, great power leaders have not taken advantage of this opportunity to strengthen their own security, reduce the economic burden of military spending, build regional security, and thus eliminate the incentives to acquire weapons of mass destruction. What these leaders need to begin exploring cooperative measures to strengthen world security is a big push from the public.

Some military and foreign policy specialists believe that actions by the international community are unlikely to have much impact one way or the other on the proliferation of weapons of mass destruction or the risks of major conventional war. Decisions on these matters, they claim, will always be made by national leaders on the basis of what they deem to be in the national interest (or in their own political interests). Experts who hold this view generally argue not that nonproliferation efforts are pernicious or counterproductive, but only that they have little proven value. The authors of this book disagree, believing that there is considerable evidence that candidate proliferators have responded to international pressure, sanctions, and incentives.

There is, however, a deeper source of disagreement: this is the view of some analysts that arms control measures limiting the nuclear or conventional military capabilities of the great powers, particularly the United States, may actually foster proliferation, rather than discourage it. The reasoning behind this idea is that as long as at least one great power "carries a big stick," potentially aggressive Third World leaders may feel constrained to accept the *status quo*; but if the threat of great power military action, particularly unfettered, unilateral action, is markedly reduced, provocative leaders may decide to use conventional force, backed up by threats of mass destruction, to advance national interests at the expense of other nations.

Actual programs undertaken by developing countries over the past several decades suggest that the opposite is true. The enormous US military build-up in the 1980s and early 1990s under Presidents Ronald Reagan and George Bush did not deter Iraq, Iran, or North Korea from launching nuclear weapon programs, nor in the case of Iraq did it deter the use of chemical weapons against Iran nor prevent a major act of conventional aggression. In China, the main impact of massive US and Russian nuclear and conventional military capabilities has been not to discourage investment in the military, but to set an ever-rising standard of military sophistication that China is constantly striving to match.

In sum, recent history suggests that positive nonproliferation strategies can induce proliferant nations to restrain from developing weapons of mass destruction and threatening to use them; policies of implicit nuclear or convention threat are unlikely to do so.

Strengthening Public Support for Nonproliferation Efforts

The sources of public opinion on issues of international security, including proliferation, are obscure. In Western industrial nations, newspapers and weekly news magazines do contain much information on the risks of nuclear proliferation and on national initiatives that might help head off this danger. But few people read much international news, and even for those who do, there are remarkably few opportunities to learn about competing national policy approaches, much less hear them debated.

As a result, government policies often become locked in patterns that serve special interests more than the general good. Since those who follow international security issues represent a small minority of the voters, politicians rely mainly on experts for guidance; experts generally limit their advice to tried and true policies that, because they are familiar, will not put office-holders at risk of any public challenge; and journalists report mainly official national policy, not competing alternatives, because the first priority of audiences with limited time for consumption is to understand current government policy. Even when vested interests are not at stake, lack of informed public debate on current and alternative policies constrains the options politicians will publicly support; and, in a circular manner, the lack of initiative by politicians perpetuates a lack of informed public education and debate.

In countries with democratic institutions, concerned citizens can break into this cycle by participating in public education projects, supporting nonprofit public interest groups, and participating in grassroots outreach activities. Through research, publications, public forums, and media interviews, public interest groups attempt to fill in the gaps left by the mass media. Such groups try to develop and publicize policy alternatives, creating a baseline for assessing and debating the pros and cons of official policies.

In the United States, many public interest groups work to strengthen current government efforts to stop the proliferation of nuclear, chemical, and biological weapons. These include two major research centers, the Carnegie Endowment for International Peace and the Brookings Institution, both of which conduct and publish extensive original research on the nature of the problem and on potential means of addressing it. The leading organizations for grassroots education and national lobbying include the Union of Concerned Scientists, the Wisconsin Project on Nuclear Arms Control, Physicians for Social Responsibility (PSR), the Nuclear Control Institute, the Lawyers Alliance for World Security, the Council for a Livable World, and the Campaign for the Nonproliferation Treaty, a coalition of other public interest groups.

Most of the grassroots groups and lobby groups are based in Washington, D.C., but many have local chapters or branches around the country. These include Peace Action (formerly Sane/Freeze) and PSR. In addition, many colleges offer undergraduate courses in international relations or peace or security studies that include a unit on nonproliferation; and faculty members often team up with local public interest groups to sponsor widely advertised public forums, in an effort to reach other students and members of the local community.

In fact, a newly concerned individual might feel a bit overwhelmed by the plethora of organizations and resources focusing on nonproliferation issues at the national level. Why are there so many groups? And why does so much energy go into holding public meetings, which at best create a larger number of moderately informed, but frustrated individuals who feel that they have no national-level influence?

As all activists know, becoming better informed and actively involved in any public policy issue is demanding and sometimes frustrating. On any important issue, there are many different public interest groups, with diverse styles of public education and organization and often with somewhat differing views on the best policy. Generally, these groups can raise more money to support their activities separately than they would if they banded together; and their distinct viewpoints offer an important range of choices to those who want to learn more, to consider the alternatives, or to become active as a member or volunteer. Of course, to benefit from the virtues of diversity, it is necessary to spend some time sampling the literature and activities of various organizations.

The constant education and outreach activities of public interest groups influence government policy in many ways, most of which can be lumped together under the simple rubric of "creating a commotion." As more and more individuals and groups express concern at the local and national levels, the scale of informal networking (talking over back fences) grows, multiplying many-fold the number of individuals who engage in discussion and debate. Ten concerned voters cannot have much impact on a member of Congress, but several hundred can get a serious hearing, because the member knows that behind each active person are five or ten like-minded individuals at home.

National campaigns and movements develop by snowballing. When enough people care about something, there is a geometrically spreading process of engaging others. At a certain scale, views that were previously marginal or "fringe" begin to be reported in the mass media. Then if large-scale concern persists, issues and policy options begin to be analyzed in the mass media in a way that can educate the electorate on a mass scale on the pros and cons of potential government policies.

Every teacher and public interest group leader working on nonproliferation issues knows that his or her actions can make a difference—if those at the receiving end are moved enough to take some independent action on their own: Writing a letter to the editor of the local newspaper or the State Department or the president. Going to the library to read more. Talking to a friend. Volunteering for a public interest group that is trying to conduct a broader education and outreach campaign.

In matters of international politics, the actions of individuals are like drops in a fast-moving river: no one person can take much credit if the course of the river changes direction, but those who linger in backwaters weaken the current for change.

The Organization and Purposes of this Primer

This book provides a comprehensive introduction to nonproliferation issues. Chapter 2 starts with the basics: What are weapons of mass destruction? What makes them different from conventional weapons? Which countries have them, may have them, or may have programs to acquire them?

Chapter 3 looks at the technologies that must be mastered before countries can produce weapons of mass destruction on their own, and it indicates where access to needed know-how and materials is readily available, and where steep hurdles lie.

Chapter 4 reviews the terms, scope, and implementation of international treaties and agreements to limit the spread of weapons of mass destruction. It gives a sense of progress to date.

Chapter 5 surveys the range of potential measures available to the international community to try to prevent the spread of weapons of mass destruction, or respond to proliferation if it occurs.

Chapter 6 highlights recent trends that favor nonproliferation or foster proliferation, and it surveys current US and international nonproliferation efforts.

Chapter 7 takes a longer-term view. It suggests some far-reaching changes in security policy that the world's leading military powers (the five nuclear weapon states) could make to minimize the risks of any further proliferation. The proposed policies would leave no stone unturned in the effort to reduce the role of nuclear weapons in international affairs, to minimize the global and regional risks of major conventional war (thereby eliminating the main incentive for acquiring weapons of mass destruction), and to maximize international pressures and incentives for nonproliferation.

The step-by-step approach of the primer should make it easy for readers to absorb the ins and outs of current proliferation issues. For readers mainly interested in information, understanding, and research, the primer provides a wealth of material, along with extensive references for further reading. For those who are already activists or seek to become more active, we hope the primer will help refine priorities and connections among seemingly disparate or competing themes or activities.

Chapter 2

Weapons of Mass Destruction

Destruction of human beings on a large scale is not new to warfare, nor even to this century. Nevertheless, weapons of mass destruction compress the amount of time and effort needed to kill. Wars lasting a few hours could now devastate populations, cities, or entire countries in ways that previously took months or years. Nuclear or biological wars among proliferant nations may not match the scope of a US-Soviet exchange of thousands of thermonuclear weapons, but the damage to their people could still be catastrophic.

Since the end of the Cold War, the proliferation of weapons of mass destruction has become much more prominent in US national security and foreign policy planning. Revelations about Iraqi, North Korean, South African, and Israeli nuclear weapon programs, the possibility of a nuclear arms race in South Asia, and the multidimensional conflicts in the Middle East all point to the urgency of the problem. Adding a dangerous new twist is the dissolution of the Soviet Union, a superpower armed with nuclear, chemical, and biological weapons whose successor states are beset by economic crises and political instability.

At least three main factors underlie this renewed emphasis on proliferation. First, the reduced military threat from the former Soviet Union has increased the relative importance of lesser powers, especially if armed with weapons of mass destruction. Second, certain international political and technological trends are increasing the threat to international security from proliferation. Third, new opportunities are opening for enhancing the current international regimes designed to stem proliferation.

Since at least the 1960s, when it sponsored the nuclear Nonproliferation Treaty (NPT), the United States has recognized that proliferation is a global problem which requires extensive international cooperation. In several cases, the United States has successfully exerted unilateral influence to discourage proliferation, and it will no doubt continue to do so. But placing a priority on nonproliferation will require the further development and enforcement of international norms and behavior. International conditions today offer significant opportunities for such cooperation.

Nuclear, Chemical, and Biological Weapons

Nuclear, chemical, and biological weapons are commonly lumped together as "weapons of mass destruction," yet their effects, relative lethalities, and military applications are very different (see Appendix Table 1). Nuclear weapons, which can be more than a million times more powerful than the same weight of conventional explosives, create blast (shock waves and high pressures), flying debris, and extreme heat—the same mechanisms by which conventional explosives injure and kill, but at a vastly increased scale. In addition, nuclear explosions create neutron and gamma radiation which can kill or harm those exposed at the instant of detonation.[1] Nuclear weapons can also generate long-term radioactivity in the form of fallout which can spread over an area much greater than that affected by blast or heat. Radioactive fallout can cause acute illness or death at great distances within minutes, hours, or days of the detonation. It can also lead to long-delayed medical problems such as cancer or genetic abnormalities.[2]

---

[1] If detonated at high altitudes, nuclear weapons can generate powerful radio waves, called "electromagnetic pulse," that wreak havoc with electronic equipment, but do not pose a direct risk to human health.

[2] In principle, nations or terrorist groups could develop radiological weapons whose effects are similar to those of radioactive fallout but over a far smaller area. Such weapons disseminate highly radioactive material using mechanical means or conventional explosives. Their effects resemble those of chemical more than nuclear weapons, since they contaminate territory and poison living organisms but do not destroy physical structures. Conventional attacks on nuclear power plants could be tantamount to radiological warfare on a much more massive scale. Although there are no documented cases of any nation trying to acquire radiological weapons, the Geneva-based UN Conference on

Chemical agents are poisons that incapacitate, injure, or kill through their toxic effects on the skin, eyes, lungs, blood, nerves, or other organs. Some chemical warfare agents can be lethal when vaporized and inhaled in amounts as small as a few milligrams.

As potent as chemical agents are, biological agents can be much deadlier, pound for pound. Biological agents are disease-causing microorganisms, such as bacteria, rickettsiae, and viruses. Laboratory tests on animals indicate that, if effectively disseminated and inhaled, ten grams of anthrax spores (a form of disease-inducing bacteria) could produce as many casualties as a ton (one million grams) of nerve agent. Some poisons, or toxins, made naturally by certain bacteria, plants, and animals are also lethal in minute quantities, and might be manufactured in a biological weapon program.

Frightening as they are, weapons of mass destruction represent only part of the world's post–Cold War security problems. Diffusion of militarily useful advanced technology, continuing conventional arms sales, and the resurgence of hitherto suppressed regional and ethnic rivalries are spurring a broader problem: the growth of advanced military capability among states and sub-national groups that are potentially hostile toward each other. Not only are weapons of mass destruction and their delivery systems spreading, but so are advanced conventional weapons, along with the equipment needed to create a command, control, communication, and intelligence infrastructure. Even simple weapons can produce massive casualties, as shown by the World War II fire bomb attacks that caused up to 100,000 deaths in Tokyo and 200,000 in Dresden. The proliferation of nuclear, chemical, and biological weapons is, nevertheless, of particular concern.

Delivery Systems

To do their deadly work, agents of mass destruction have to be integrated into weapons (e.g., an aerial bomb, a ballistic missile warhead, or even a suitcase) and delivered to their targets. Such weapons can be highly threatening even without sophisticated delivery systems. A

Disarmament theoretically includes radiological weapons on its agenda. Sweden has proposed including attacks on nuclear facilities under this rubric, while the United States, France, and Germany favor limiting the talks to traditional radiological weapons.

nuclear device planted by a terrorist or commando squad, or delivered by a disguised cargo ship, civil aircraft, or even a small pleasure boat, can kill just as many people as one delivered by intercontinental ballistic missile; a given quantity of certain lethal microorganisms would probably kill even more people if spread effectively by human agents than if by a missile. In the cases of rival states bordering each other, weapons of mass destruction mounted on even short-range means of delivery can pose a major threat.

Nevertheless, states able to couple weapons of mass destruction to delivery systems with longer ranges, or a greater ability to penetrate defenses, can threaten more nations with higher levels of destruction, and with greater likelihood of success. At the same time, since such delivery systems—taken here to be ballistic missiles, cruise missiles, and combat aircraft—generally pose greater technical challenges, they are more amenable to international controls than less sophisticated delivery systems.

Of these three delivery systems, ballistic missiles have attracted the most attention, both because they are difficult to defend against and because they appear to be particularly suited for weapons of mass destruction. (When armed with conventional warheads, they generally do not have a military value proportionate to their cost, although they can have considerable political significance.) Combat aircraft also pose a potent threat for the delivery of mass-destruction weapons. They are far more widely available than missiles with a comparable combat radius, and efforts to control their spread are greatly complicated by the multiple roles that aircraft play. Cruise missiles and other unmanned aerial vehicles could also be used to deliver weapons of mass destruction, but cruise missiles with the ranges and payloads typical of combat aircraft and ballistic missiles are not yet widely available.

The Potential for Mass Destruction

What differentiates weapons of mass destruction from conventional weapons are the large scale and indiscriminate nature of the effects of the former, particularly against civilians. Mass-destruction weapons make it possible for a single missile or airplane to kill as many people as thousands of planeloads of conventional weaponry. Such weapons can give states or sub-national groups the ability to inflict damage that is wholly disproportionate to their conventional military capabilities or to the nature of the conflict in which they are used.

"Mass destruction" is a relative term. The fire bomb attacks on Dresden killed between 130,000 and 200,000 people with 1,400 aircraft sorties over two days. The single atomic bomb dropped on Hiroshima immediately killed an estimated 68,000 people and injured another 76,000. A hydrogen bomb exploding over Detroit might kill 470,000 and injure 630,000 more. Thus, a single weapon of mass destruction can do damage equivalent to that of hundreds or thousands of conventional high explosive or incendiary weapons.

Nuclear weapons with high yields are the most potent means of mass destruction. A small one-kiloton nuclear blast releases the energy of 1,000 *tons* of conventional high explosives; the energy of a large one-megaton blast equals that of 1,000,000 tons of high explosives, or 1,000 kilotons. In addition to instantly killing tens of thousands, hundreds of thousands, or millions of people, a single very large nuclear weapon can obliterate the entire physical infrastructure of a large city and contaminate a much larger area with radioactive fallout. According to the "nuclear winter" hypothesis, a war in which hundreds or thousands of nuclear weapons were detonated could put enough fine dust and smoke into the atmosphere to block the sun and cause subfreezing temperatures even in summer, leading to widespread agricultural failure and mass starvation.[3] (At present, only the declared nuclear weapon states have arsenals large enough to produce a nuclear winter.)

Biological weapons are so potent that under conditions favorable to the attacker, they can kill as many people as comparably-sized nuclear weapons, potentially making them extremely dangerous as a strategic or terrorist weapon against dense population centers. Pound for pound, chemical weapons are less lethal than nuclear or biological weapons, and correspondingly greater amounts would be needed to have comparable results (see Figures 1 and 2). Indeed, it may not be appropriate to consider them to be weapons of mass destruction. Yet they can induce terror, particularly among troops or civilians without protective gear.

Because weapons of mass destruction are compact relative to their destructive power, they can be delivered far more easily than conventional weapons with comparable effects. For example, a nuclear

---

[3] R.P. Turco, O.B. Toon, T.P. Ackerman, J.B. Pollack, and Carl Sagan, "Nuclear Winter: Global Consequences of Multiple Nuclear Explosions," *Science*, Volume 222, No. 4630 (December 23, 1983), pp. 1283–1292.

Figure 1: Comparing Lethal Areas of Chemical, Biological, and Nuclear Weapons: Missile Delivery on an Overcast Day or Night, With Moderate Wind (Neither Best nor Worst Case)

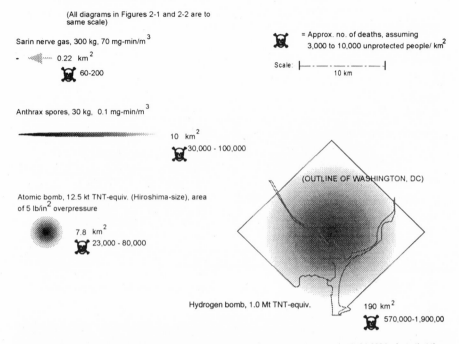

(All diagrams in Figures 2-1 and 2-2 are to same scale)

Sarin nerve gas, 300 kg, 70 mg-min/m^3

0.22 km^2

60-200

= Approx. no. of deaths, assuming 3,000 to 10,000 unprotected people/ km^2

Scale: 10 km

Anthrax spores, 30 kg, 0.1 mg-min/m^3

10 km^2

30,000 - 100,000

Atomic bomb, 12.5 kt TNT-equiv. (Hiroshima-size), area of 5 lb/in^2 overpressure

7.8 km^2

23,000 - 80,000

(OUTLINE OF WASHINGTON, DC)

Hydrogen bomb, 1.0 Mt TNT-equiv.

190 km^2

570,000-1,900,00

Figure shows the lethal areas of the agents delivered by a Scud-like missile with a maximum payload of 1,000 kg (note that the amount of biological weapon agent assumed would weigh considerably less than this; since the lethality per unit weight is great, the smaller amount considered here would still more than cover a large urban area). The estimates of lethal areas for chemical and biological weapons were prepared using a model that takes account of postulated release height, wind velocity, deposition velocity, height of temperature inversion layer, urban air currents, and residence time in air of the agent. The diagrams show approximate outer contours of areas with sufficient concentrations of agent that 50 percent to 100 percent of the unprotected people would receive fatal doses. Although some people within the defined area would survive, about the same number in the outer, less lethal areas, would die; therefore, the defined areas give approximations of the total number of unprotected people who could be expected to die in each scenario. With ideal (for lethality) population densities and weather, the chemical and biological agents could kill more people than shown here; under worse conditions, they might kill many fewer. The atomic weapons (fission and fusion) are assumed to be air burst for optimum blast and radiation effects, producing little lethal fallout. The lethal area is assumed to be that receiving 5 lb/in^2 of overpressure—enough to level wood or unreinforced brick houses.

WEAPONS OF MASS DESTRUCTION | 17

weapon that can destroy a city can be delivered in a truck. With the right weather, a single aircraft can disseminate high doses of a biological agent over hundreds, or even thousands, of square kilometers by spraying a long line upwind from the target region.

Nuclear weapons delivered by ballistic missile or by unconventional means (for example, a truck) are particularly difficult to defend against. Biological and chemical weapons are also difficult to defend against if their presence is unknown. Evacuation is the best defense against all of these weapons, if there is enough warning. Otherwise, special defensive equipment—sealed buildings or special masks and clothing—are needed for defense against chemical and biological weapons. For nuclear weapons, shelters can offer varying degrees of protection outside the central destructive area of the bomb.

Massively destructive weapons can alter international balances of power in diverse ways. If armed with such weapons, a relatively small nation may gain useful leverage against a larger nation or more numerous adversaries. France's primary argument for acquiring its nuclear *force de frappe* was that although a French nuclear blow would be limited in comparison to the damage that the Soviet Union could inflict, it might still impose a higher price on aggression than the Soviets would find worthwhile. Israel seems to believe that its undeclared nuclear weapons give it an ultimate deterrent against invasion by its more numerous Arab neighbors. In the hands of an aggressor, nuclear weapons might be used to deter resistance to aggression.

During the Cold War, when the United States interacted with a Soviet Union heavily armed with nuclear, chemical, and possibly biological weapons aimed at US territory, US forces abroad, and US allies, this constrained US definitions of its national interests, its policies for defending those interests, and its strategies and tactics for managing clashes of interest.

Would other, smaller nuclear (or biological or chemical) arsenals deter the United States from conventional regional intervention to protect its interests? Possibly. In the Gulf War, the United States was concerned about but not deterred from intervention by Iraq's known chemical arsenal and possible biological weapons. If Iraq had been able to threaten to use even a small number of nuclear weapons against US cities or the territory of US allies, the calculus of US intervention would have been different. US decisions might then have depended on whether US leaders believed that Iraq's leaders would have been

Figure 2: Comparing Lethal Areas of Chemical and Biological Weapons: Delivery by Aircraft as Aerosol Line Source

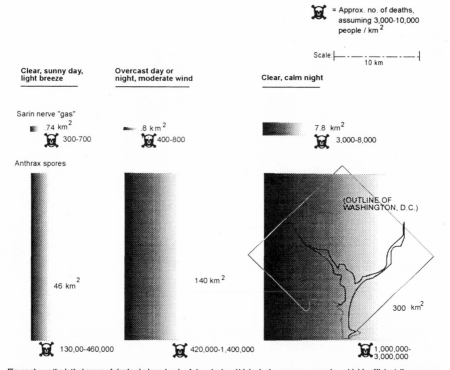

Figure shows the lethal areas of single airplane-loads of chemical and biological weapons, assuming a highly efficient, line-source delivery of the killing agents. The figure also assumes that the aircraft has a greater payload than the missile in figure 2-1, delivering 1,000 kg of sarin nerve agent or 100 kg of anthrax spores. (More anthrax would be inefficient in a city attack.) **Given these two factors, a single airplane delivering chemical or biological weapons can be considerably more lethal than a single missile.** For an anthrax attack, the diagram shows how fatalities could vary greatly under three different weather scenarios. In one case, that of an overcast day or night with moderate wind, maximizing the lethal area would require distributing the agent in a 4.5 km by 34 km area, which would not be appropriate for most cities; therefore, the figure assumes a more rectangular distribution, which would still generate a comparable number of casualties.

deterred from escalating to the use of nuclear weapons by US nuclear retaliatory capabilities.

In one historical case the proliferant nation hoped to use its nuclear weapons not to deter US military intervention, but to cause it. In a 1993 speech, South African President F.W. de Klerk said that in the 1980s, South Africa's "strategy was that if the situation in southern Africa were to deteriorate seriously, a confidential indication of the nuclear deterrent capability would be given to one or more of the major powers, for example the United States, in an attempt to persuade them to intervene."[4] Thus, South Africa hoped to engage in a kind of reverse nuclear blackmail.

One concern of the Cold War was the European fear that the superpowers would fight a so-called "tactical" nuclear war in Europe—with consequences for Europe as terrible as a "strategic" nuclear exchange would have been for the United States and the Soviet Union. In that case, however, the United States shared at least some risk of nuclear devastation with its allies. In future confrontations with proliferant nuclear powers lacking the means to attack the United States, US regional allies would bear heavier relative risks of nuclear attack from the proliferant state, and they might be reluctant to do so. Some states facing a regional nuclear-armed adversary might welcome an alliance with a major nuclear power—if they believed that this would help deter conventional aggression or nuclear threats by the adversary. But such a deterrent threat might not be fully credible.

Threats Posed by Proliferation

Proliferation poses dangers to all nations. The states now working hardest to develop weapons of mass destruction are for the most part located in unstable regions of the world—the Middle East, South Asia, and the Korean peninsula—where bitter, unresolved rivalries have erupted into war in the past and could do so again. New deployments of weapons of mass destruction in these regions could exacerbate tensions and pose heightened risks of their use in time of war.

---

[4] President F.W. de Klerk, speech to joint session of the South African Parliament, transcribed from Johannesburg Radio South Africa Network, March 24, 1993 (Foreign Broadcast Information Service (FBIS)-JPRS-TND-93-009, March 29, 1993, p.2).

For at least the next decade, few if any of these states will be able to deliver such weapons more than about 1,000 km (620 miles) in a reliable and timely manner. Therefore, the greatest threat posed by these states is to their neighbors and to regional stability. Despite their lack of access to intercontinental delivery systems, proliferant states can in principle threaten any country on earth using unconventional means of delivery, such as covert or disguised ships or trucks.

The breakup of the Soviet Union presents several threats to the global nonproliferation regime.[5] One possibility is that Belarus, Kazakhstan, or Ukraine will renege on their commitments to return all the nuclear warheads on their territories to Russia. Recent developments in this area have been positive, however. All three nations have joined the NPT as non-nuclear weapon states and have begun to transfer warheads to Russia under the terms of mutually agreed schedules. If any of these nations were to suspend their cooperation, that would seriously undermine nonproliferation efforts. Another danger is the leakage of nuclear weapon materials or actual weapons to potential proliferants elsewhere in the world if the nuclear custodial system in Russia itself were to break down. Yet another concern is the export from former Soviet republics of equipment, technology, or expertise relevant to producing weapons of mass destruction. A wide range of additional dangers could arise from the possible development of an authoritarian government in Russia itself.

A few analysts, pointing to the role that nuclear weapons seem to have played in preventing an East-West war, argue that the spread of such weapons will actually increase international stability. Most, however, consider such a view dangerously misguided. The Cold War was not without serious crises and close calls, such as the Cuban Missile Crisis. In the Middle East, South Asia, and the Korean peninsula, hostile powers share common borders, contest core values and vital national interests, and lack the mutual learning experience and technical safeguards that have helped the superpowers control the mortal threat each poses to the other.

Proliferation poses particular problems for US foreign policy. As a global power, the United States will almost certainly retain allies and interests overseas that might be threatened by states possessing weapons of mass destruction. Should the United States seek to defend

---

[5] This regime comprises the treaties and agreements described in Chapter 4 and the export controls described in Chapters 5 and 6.

these interests with military force—whether acting unilaterally or under multilateral auspices such as those of the United Nations—US armed forces or territory might become targets for weapons of mass destruction. And if new countries acquire nuclear weapons with which to threaten US allies, US forces overseas, or even US territory, the US government will have to reassess the conditions under which it will risk nuclear attack.

Plausible scenarios in which the current set of suspected proliferants might threaten US territory with nuclear or other weapons of mass destruction are difficult to devise. None possesses missiles or aircraft with sufficient range to reach the United States, and none is likely to obtain such systems in the next decade. Nevertheless, a state that badly wanted to wreak destruction on a US city could probably do so, whether or not it had long-range missiles (and, obviously, whether or not the United States had defenses against such missiles).

One likely result of proliferation is more proliferation. India justifies its nuclear weapon program by pointing to China's. Pakistan has tried to keep up with India. Iran may have decided it must match Iraq's chemical weapons, as well as try to develop nuclear weapons. Some Arab nations have sought nuclear weapons to counter those of Israel, or they may have pursued biological weapons as the "poor man's atomic bomb." If proliferation proceeds, more nations that until now have forgone the nuclear option may reconsider. For example, if North Korea got nuclear weapons, South Korea might be strongly tempted to follow suit, particularly if it believed that US security guarantees and involvement in Pacific affairs were weakening. Japan, too, might question its renunciation of nuclear weapons.

In addition, more states in the business of making nuclear, chemical, or biological weapons could mean more potential suppliers of the means of production or actual weapons to still other parties—perhaps states, perhaps terrorist groups. Even if proliferant states did not intentionally transfer these goods, they might become targets for illicit foreign purchasers and smugglers.

In the worst case, the actual use of weapons of mass destruction would undermine nonproliferation norms. Iraq's use of chemical weapons has already weakened the international taboo attached to them. The first large-scale use of biological weapons would be shocking, the next less so, and so on. Moreover, a single successful application of a biological weapon might inspire non-state terrorists to try the same thing.

Although use of a few nuclear weapons might mobilize the international community into action to prevent a recurrence, it might instead show that outside powers will try to keep their distance. For this reason, the fewer the countries that have weapons of mass destruction, the better are the chances that international norms against their use will be upheld.

This book does not address the potential terrorist uses of weapons of mass destruction.[6] But any nation building such weapons must erect and maintain a formidable security apparatus, both to protect the secrets of the weapons and to prevent their falling into unauthorized hands. Ineffective or inexperienced governments, especially those with relatively unstable regimes, may not be as successful at ensuring control as have the current owners of nuclear, chemical, or biological weapon facilities. Indeed, it is still too early to be certain that Russia will successfully gain and keep stable, central control over all the weapons and fissile material of the former Soviet Union.

The disintegration of national political authority, regional secession, or civil war could deliver weapons of mass destruction into the hands of groups that, at best, would be poorly equipped to manage the weapons safely. Again, the republics of the former Soviet Union, perhaps including Russia, seem vulnerable to this risk.

The start-up costs of a nuclear weapon program are great. Iraq probably spent about $10 billion before its efforts were interrupted. A narrower program than Iraq's might cost less, but could still cost billions. Acquisition programs for chemical and biological weapons cost much less. Despite the expense, some countries may see weapons of mass destruction as substitutes for larger, even more expensive, conventional forces, just as the United States decided in the 1950s that nuclear weapons were a way of getting "more bang for the buck." In most cases the quest for weapons of mass destruction is embedded in an across-the-board arms competition feeding regional arms races. Nations pay for these arms races at the cost of their peoples' welfare.

The development of weapons of mass destruction has caused environmental damage. The United States and the former Soviet Union face monstrous clean-up operations at facilities where nuclear weapons were manufactured: radioactive elements and hazardous chemicals contam-

---

[6] For more information on these uses, see US Congress, Office of Technology Assessment, *Technology Against Terrorism: Structuring Security*, OTA-ISC-511 (Washington, D.C.: US Government Printing Office, January 1992).

inate the soil, sediments, surface water, and ground water at most or all of the sites. Completing the US cleanup could cost hundreds of billions of dollars. Little is known about the public health consequences if the mess is not cleaned up—as may happen for economic reasons in the former Soviet Union.

Production and destruction of chemical weapons also pose environmental risks. In part because of citizen concerns, neither the United States nor Russia has finalized plans (let alone built the facilities) to destroy its chemical weapons according to the 10-year schedule set out in the Chemical Weapons Convention. The recklessness with which Iraq's chemical weapon program handled toxic chemicals (as reported by UN Special Commission inspectors) illustrates another problem: Developing nations manufacturing weapons of mass destruction are unlikely to allocate scarce resources to environmental health and safety.

Infectious biological agents eventually die, and toxins are biodegradable. But some spore-forming microorganisms, in particular anthrax bacteria, can persist in the environment for many years. Moreover, biological weapon programs themselves can pose a threat to public health, as apparently happened when anthrax spores were accidentally released in 1979 from a biological weapon research facility in the Soviet city of Sverdlovsk, triggering a deadly epidemic.

Nations with Nuclear, Chemical, or Biological Weapon Programs

NATIONS WITH ACKNOWLEDGED NUCLEAR, CHEMICAL, OR BIOLOGICAL PROGRAMS

Five countries—the United States, Russia, France, China, and Great Britain—openly acknowledge possessing stocks of nuclear weapons. As noted earlier, three Soviet successor states—Belarus, Kazakhstan, and Ukraine—also have former Soviet strategic nuclear weapons on their territory, but have become non-nuclear weapon states under the NPT. In 1992, when they signed the Lisbon Protocol to the Strategic Arms Reduction Treaty (START), all three agreed to transfer the nuclear warheads on their territory to Russia by the end of START's seven-year weapon reduction period, ending in 2001.

The nuclear weapon arsenals of France, China, and Britain are estimated at 417, 300, and 196, respectively.[7] The arsenals of the United States and Russia are much larger. Under the terms of the START II agreement, which has not yet been ratified, US and Russian treaty-accountable warheads would be limited to no more than 3,500 each.[8] In addition to this figure for warheads on strategic intercontinental systems, both countries have many thousands of nuclear warheads previously deployed on shorter-range systems. The latter have been withdrawn from front-line deployment, but are still part of the stored arsenal on the two sides.[9]

Only three states, the United States, Russia, and Iraq, say that they have had chemical weapons; and in these cases, the weapons have been destroyed, are in the process of being destroyed, or are slated for destruction. No country admits to having biological weapon programs—only, at most, programs for defense against such weapons.[10] In all, then, only five countries overtly deploy or possess weapons of mass destruction: the five acknowledged nuclear weapon states.

NATIONS WITH COVERT NUCLEAR WEAPON PROGRAMS

The difficulty in assessing the extent of the proliferation threat lies in determining which states are developing weapons of mass destruction in secret. Counting all states capable of mounting a program to produce weapons of mass destruction would inflate the proliferation threat, just as counting only states that acknowledge such programs errs in the opposite direction.

In addition to the acknowledged nuclear weapon states, three "threshold states" appear to either possess nuclear weapons or have the ability to deploy them on short notice. They are Israel, which is widely believed to have a clandestine arsenal; India, which tested a nuclear device in 1974 and probably has stockpiles of nuclear weapon material available, but has made no overt moves to develop a nuclear

---

[7] Selig Harrison, "Zero Nuclear Weapons. Zero," *New York Times*, February 15, 1995, p. A21.

[8] *Arms Control Reporter*, 1995, pp. 614.A.1–4.

[9] *Arms Control Reporter*, 1992, pp. 408.E.17–32.

[10] Russia has admitted that the Soviet Union's offensive biological weapon program persisted after the USSR signed the Biological Weapon Convention banning such work, but insists that this program has since been halted. The United States, Russia, France, the United Kingdom, and Canada admit having had offensive biological weapon supplies or development programs in the past.

arsenal; and Pakistan, which is cut off from US military aid because the president cannot certify that it does not possess a nuclear explosive device.[11] None of these countries is a party to the NPT.

South Africa has admitted to mounting a nuclear weapon program that culminated in the construction of six nuclear weapons. However, stating that it has destroyed those weapons, it has since joined the NPT as a non-nuclear weapon state and opened up its nuclear facilities to international inspection. Little information has been released so far on the results of those inspections, but the International Atomic Energy Agency (IAEA) has praised South Africa for its cooperation in documenting its past program and in establishing a safeguards regime.

A few other states reputed to have nuclear weapon programs are apparently not as far advanced as the above four: Iran and Libya, both long-time NPT members; North Korea, which announced its intention to withdraw from the NPT in 1993 and then reversed this position; and possibly Algeria, which recently acceded to the NPT.

Over the past two years, North Korea has raised more concern than any other potential proliferant. After signing the NPT in late 1985, North Korea refused to sign an IAEA safeguards agreement, as required by the NPT, until early 1992. When North Korea permitted the IAEA to conduct several inspections of declared facilities in 1992 and early 1993, the agency discovered a number of discrepancies between the amount of nuclear material North Korea declared and the amount indicated by agency testing. The IAEA asked to inspect two undeclared sites it suspected of containing wastes from a nuclear fuel reprocessing facility, but North Korea denied access to the sites, saying they were military sites that had no nuclear role. Determined to avoid another situation like that in Iraq (discussed below), the IAEA invoked its right to conduct a "special inspection" of the two suspicious sites. North Korea responded in March 1993 by announcing its intention to withdraw from the NPT, the first nation ever to do so.

North Korea's withdrawal notice spurred bilateral talks between North Korea and the United States over the next 18 months, culminating in an agreement under which North Korea will remain in the NPT. In the "Agreed Framework" signed by the two nations in October

---

[11] On August 23, 1994, former Pakistani Primer Minister Nawaz Sharit announced that "Pakistan possesses the atomic bomb." This statement was the most definitive yet made by such a high-ranking official. *Arms Control Reporter*, 1994, p. 452.B.204.

1994, North Korea agreed to remain a party to the treaty, to accept full-scope IAEA safeguards, and to dismantle its existing nuclear facilities. In return, the United States promised to organize an international consortium, led by South Korea, to build in North Korea two modern, light-water moderated nuclear power reactors with a design less useful for producing materials for nuclear weapons and much easier to safeguard. This agreement, the terms of which are to be fulfilled by 2003, is now in the earliest stages of implementation, and there is great uncertainty over how smoothly future developments will proceed. For example, North Korea has said it might not allow the IAEA to inspect the two suspected waste sites until construction of the new reactors has been completed. The United States will doubtless seek an earlier inspection.

Iraq's programs to build weapons of mass destruction constitute another worrisome case. Following the 1991 Gulf War, the United Nations imposed a rigorous program of dismantling all of Iraq's nuclear, chemical, and biological weapons and the facilities to produce them. While implementing this program, the United Nations discovered that Iraq's nuclear program was broader and more advanced than Western intelligence agencies had suspected. By UN estimates, Iraq was 18–24 months away from producing a nuclear bomb when the Gulf War started. Previously an NPT member in good standing, Iraq had successfully split its nuclear weapon program off from the declared nuclear facilities inspected by the IAEA. Iraq's success in obtaining the equipment and materials needed to build a nuclear bomb dramatically illustrates the failure of export controls as well as regular IAEA inspections to prevent proliferation.[12] Although Iraq's nuclear weapon program is now completely reversed, most observers believe that Iraq would resume the program if the United Nations were to relax its monitoring system.

In the past, Argentina and Brazil were thought to be pursuing nuclear weapon programs, but recently the two countries have agreed to open

---

[12] Dozens of corporations, primarily in West Germany, other European countries, and the United States, made a total of 240 known business deals to supply Iraq with technology needed for its nuclear and missile programs. A press report noted that "the vast majority of these deals were approved by or made through governments." Douglas Jehl, "Who Armed Iraq? Answers the West Didn't Want to Hear," *New York Times*, July 18, 1993, p. E5, based on information compiled by the Washington-based Wisconsin Project on Nuclear Arms Control.

up their nuclear facilities to bilateral and international inspection to assure each other and the rest of the world that they are not. They have also brought into force a Latin American nuclear-weapon-free zone (see Chapter 4), and Argentina recently acceded to the NPT.

NATIONS WITH COVERT CHEMICAL OR BIOLOGICAL WEAPON PROGRAMS

Public reports of potential chemical and biological proliferants diverge more than do published assessments of nuclear proliferation. The US Congressional Office of Technology Assessment has compiled a list of candidates that appear in most other published lists (see Figure 3).[13] Eight nations are suspected of having chemical *and* biological weapon programs: China, Iran, Iraq, Israel, Libya, North Korea, Syria, and Taiwan. In addition, Egypt, Myanmar (Burma), and Vietnam are suspected of possessing chemical weapons. Russia has ostensibly ended its biological weapon program, but since doubts remain about whether the program has been totally eliminated, it could be argued that Russia should be on the list.

NATIONS WITH ACCESS TO DELIVERY SYSTEMS

Most of the states listed in Figure 3 have bought or developed simple ballistic missiles with at least the capability of Scud missiles, that is, a range of 300–600 km (190–370 miles). Soviet exports of Scud-B missiles in the 1970s and 1980s played a major role in their spread. More recently, China has entered the missile market, reportedly exporting M-9 (600 km) and M-11 (300 km) missiles to Syria and Pakistan. In addition, North Korea has exported Scud-C (600 km) missiles to Iran and Syria. China has also helped Iraq to develop indigenous missile production capabilities.[14]

All of the potential proliferants except Burma have fighter-bomber aircraft, most with ranges of 1,000 km (620 miles) or more and payloads of 3,000–8,800 kg (6,600–19,400 pounds)—characteristics that would permit them to deliver weapons of mass destruction. Figure 4 shows delivery systems possessed by nations of proliferation concern.

Cruise missiles with ranges over 100 km (60 miles) are not yet common outside the overt nuclear weapon states. Israel and Taiwan have

---

[13] Figure 3 excludes the acknowledged nuclear and chemical weapon powers, discussed earlier.
[14] *Arms Control Reporter,* 1994, pp. 706.E.1–8.

Figure 3: Countries Suspected of Having Programs to Develop Weapons of Mass Destruction

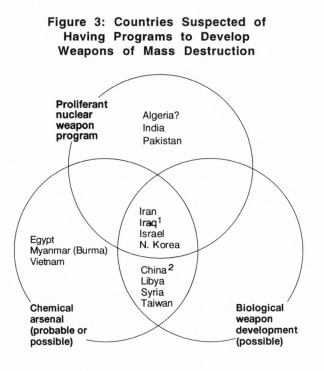

Proliferant nuclear weapon program

Algeria?
India
Pakistan

Iran
Iraq[1]
Israel
N. Korea

Egypt
Myanmar (Burma)
Vietnam

China[2]
Libya
Syria
Taiwan

Chemical arsenal (probable or possible)

Biological weapon development (possible)

[1] Iraqi programs reversed by U.N.
[2] China is an acknowledged nuclear-weapon state.

developed cruise missiles with ranges over 300 km (180 miles), but neither seems to have adapted these missiles for delivering weapons of mass destruction. The spread of relevant technologies, including the Global Positioning System, a highly accurate navigation aid, does, however, make cruise missiles a longer-term source of concern.

Potential missile holders that might want to attack the United States—countries such as Iran, Iraq, North Korea, or Libya—will not be able to field intercontinental ballistic missiles within a decade, if then, while countries which could conceivably acquire the capability—such as Israel, India, or Taiwan—are unlikely to want to do so. It is therefore unlikely that any country other than China or Russia (or, possibly, Ukraine, Kazakhstan, or Belarus) will pose a missile threat to the United States in the near- to medium-term future.

Israel and India, both suspected nuclear weapon powers, have space launch vehicles that could be adapted to serve as intercontinental ballistic missiles. Both have also tested ballistic missiles at ranges that could reach the territory of other nuclear powers: Russia in the case of Israel, and China in the case of India, posing an implicit nuclear threat and possibly provoking counter-threats.

Taiwan and South Korea do not appear to be aggressively pursuing either ballistic missile or space-launch vehicle programs at the present time, although they have the technological base to do so if they chose. Brazil's space-launch rocket program is in abeyance for financial reasons, but its level of technology gives it missile-making potential.

Practically all these countries, however, depend on assistance or purchases of supplies from abroad. Except for the most industrially advanced countries, only Israel, India, and China are arguably independent in longer-range missile design and production.

More than 40 developing countries possess antiship cruise missiles with ranges typically under 150 km (90 miles). So far, there have been no publicly identified programs among proliferant nations to develop cruise missiles for delivering weapons of mass destruction. Rather than indigenously develop long-range cruise missiles, proliferant states seeking them will most likely attempt either to attach warheads to previously unarmed systems, such as small, remotely-piloted aircraft, or to retrofit imported missiles that had originally been equipped with conventional warheads.

Since both nuclear and biological weapons carry so much destructive potential in such small packages, they are both capable of being

Figure 4: Proliferants' Delivery Systems: Selected Aircraft and Missiles

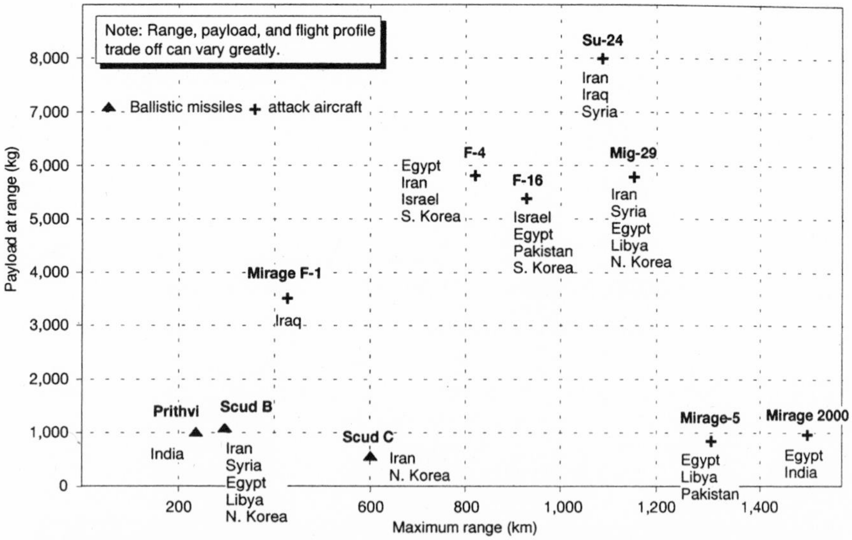

This figure shows nominal ranges and payloads of selected aircraft and missile systems of countries (beyond the 5 nuclear-weapon states) suspected of having or trying to acquire weapons of mass destruction. The graph is not intended to be exhaustive, but only to indicate that each country already possesses aircraft or missile systems of one kind or another that could be adapted to deliver weapons of mass destruction.

employed in devastating small-scale attacks initiated by unconventional means, such as smuggling and secret emplacement, or delivery by small boat or light aircraft.

In all, 14 countries, in addition to the five acknowledged nuclear powers, are widely believed to possess or to be pursuing nuclear, chemical, or biological weapons (Figure 3). Given official US government statements that "more than 25 countries...may have or may be developing" weapons of mass destruction and their delivery systems,[15] this estimate may understate the number of countries with such programs. Some of the discrepancy may involve states that are pursuing delivery systems but not nuclear, chemical, or biological weapons. In addition, there may be some countries suspected by US intelligence of pursuing weapons of mass destruction, which have not yet been identified in open sources.

Three features stand out in the overview of potential proliferants given in Figure 3. First, the estimate for the number of states pursuing nuclear weapons is relatively small—smaller than it might have been a few years ago. Second, the set of countries seeking nuclear weapons overlaps considerably with the set suspected of having chemical or biological weapon programs. Third, apart from the threat posed by former Soviet republics, the most immediate and serious risks of proliferation are concentrated in three regions of international rivalry: the Koreas, India-Pakistan, and the Middle East. Thus, on the one hand, proliferation is still sufficiently limited to warrant hope that it can be contained; on the other hand, it is occurring in places where major conflicts seriously impede nonproliferation efforts.

Assessments of longer-term risks are harder to make, although some trends are clear. For example, it is likely that only China and Russia will pose a ballistic missile threat to the territory of the United States for the next decade or longer. (Britain and France, with submarine-launched ballistic missiles capable of reaching the United States, are not considered to pose a threat.)

The probable future number of countries with nuclear, chemical, or biological weapons is elusive. It is hard to determine even the present status and likely rate of progress of existing programs. Even with the wealth of information that has been uncovered about the Iraqi nuclear weapon program, for example, experts disagree over how long it would

---

[15] Testimony of R. James Woolsey, Director of the Central Intelligence Agency, before the Senate Committee on Governmental Affairs, February 25, 1993.

Table 1: Possible Motivations for Nuclear Proliferation

Category	Motive
Military power	Deter nuclear attack
	Redress conventional arms asymmetries with rivals
	Seek military superiority over rivals
	Anticipate or match nuclear weapons of rivals
	Intimidate neighbors or rivals
	Deter intervention by extra-regional powers
International political status	Enhance regional political status
	Enhance global status
	Enhance image of technical prowess
Domestic politics	National pride or morale
	Satisfy military groups
Economic improvement	Scientific, technological or industrial spinoffs

have taken Iraq to assemble a working weapon. Moreover, extrapolating from current trends can be misleading. As noted above, there have been several examples of apparent reversal of nuclear weapon programs. Finally, further changes in the world situation, including those that nonproliferation policies seek to bring about, will affect the extent of future proliferation.

Military Roles and Other Incentives for Proliferation

The appeal of weapons of mass destruction may lie in the international status they seem to confer, their deterrent value, or their perceived utility in warfare. (Table 1 lists potential motives for nuclear proliferation.) Nuclear weapons are associated with great power status. The five permanent members of the UN Security Council are all nuclear powers, and show no sign of relinquishing that status. Nuclear weapons played multiple deterrent roles during the Cold War. Their sheer destructive power makes them attractive to military planners. Even so, the apparent commitment of the United States and Russia to make dramatic cuts in their nuclear forces is a step in the direction of decreasing the symbolic role of nuclear weapons in international affairs.

Chemical and biological weapon programs are more likely to be influenced by considerations of military utility than by other factors. These weapons do not seem to hold much attraction as symbols of international status or national pride. Nor do leaders of developing nations argue that they must pursue these weapons to enhance technical or industrial development. Some nations may see chemical or biological weapons as instruments that might be used to dominate military rivals. Some may seek such weapons to deter their use by others. Still others may see chemical or biological weapons as a "poor man's atomic bomb," with the possible roles of deterring nuclear neighbors, conventionally superior neighbors, or intervening great powers.

Among delivery systems, ballistic missiles are perceived as a symbol of technological and military prowess. The chances seem slim of building an international consensus that the status of current ballistic missile powers should be "grandfathered," like that of nuclear weapon states, while further missile proliferation is stopped. More likely, although not a near-term prospect, is a global ban on such delivery systems. Agreements to forgo or reduce ballistic missiles, if instituted at all, will probably be made in the context of regional security and arms control arrangements.

MILITARY ROLES OF NUCLEAR WEAPONS

Threatening both population and property, nuclear weapons are the most dangerous strategic weapons. While civil defense measures can mitigate their effects somewhat, within a certain radius (dependent on the explosive yield) they promise certain destruction of all but deeply buried blast shelters. Despite the great uncertainties in calculating the precise consequences of nuclear war, the impact of even a "small" or "limited" nuclear attack would be enormous.

Between World Wars I and II, the military theorist Giulio Douhet and others developed an idea of strategic bombing in which aerial attacks on key military and economic targets in the enemy's homeland would severely diminish its ability to make war. During World War II, strategic bombing evolved in practice into efforts not only to inflict crippling damage on the enemy's infrastructure, but to cripple its war effort by demoralizing the population. Although the strictly military and economic effects of the two atom bombs dropped on Japan had little direct effect on Japan's armed forces, the shock of the attacks, combined with the fear that more might follow, led to an immediate unconditional surrender.

During the Cold War, the nuclear standoff between the United States and the Soviet Union was sometimes called the "balance of terror." Although both superpowers integrated nuclear weapons into their military forces, the primary role of the weapons was not to be used in warfare, but to back up threats, that is, to deter the use of conventional force by other nations and to deter interference by other nations with their own uses of conventional force.

MILITARY ROLES OF CHEMICAL AND BIOLOGICAL WEAPONS

Medium- to large-scale attacks with chemical weapons (tens of tons) could kill unprotected people numbering in the thousands, that is, many more than would be killed with an equivalent amount of high explosives. But the many uncertainties involved in dispersing chemical agents and the effectiveness of relatively simple civil defense measures—wearing gas masks and remaining inside living spaces that are sealed off during attacks—could keep casualties relatively low. Contamination of certain areas by persistent chemical agents might slow down industrial activities for days or weeks, but for the most part the use of chemical weapons would leave the physical infrastructure of cities intact.

Chemical weapons may be used in warfare to kill or terrorize instantly, or to impede enemy operations by contaminating key areas or equipment for hours or days. In attacking an opposing infantry position, the attacker might use a volatile agent that would disperse quickly, whereas in attacking an air base or a strip of territory, the attack might employ a viscous, persistent agent.

Iraq used chemical weapons in the Iran-Iraq war with impunity and with some military success, albeit against poorly defended troops and undefended civilians. In addition, in 1990 Saddam Hussein attempted to invoke the deterrent value of chemical weapons by threatening to use them in response to Israeli nuclear threats or other (undefined) acts of Israeli aggression. Many in the Arab world defended this Iraqi threat against Western criticism. It remains to be understood why Iraq did not use chemical weapons in the Gulf War. It also remains to be seen what lessons potential chemical weapon proliferants will draw from the ultimate inability of Iraq's threat to use chemical weapons to save it from catastrophic military defeat.

Like chemical weapons, biological weapons would leave the material (as opposed to human) economic and military infrastructure of a given area relatively untouched.[16] Like nuclear weapons, biological weapons have the potential in modest amounts (a few kilograms), optimally delivered, to kill or disable many thousands of urban residents and seriously impair war-supporting activities. Unlike nuclear or chemical agents, however, biological weapons (except for some toxins) tend to act slowly, taking days or weeks to achieve their full effect. Moreover, the effects of biological weapons—like those of chemical weapons, but unlike those of nuclear weapons—can be hard to predict: weather, time of day, local terrain, and civil defense measures could all have a significant impact on casualties.

For biological weapons, there is little documented experience with military use. One analyst speculates that for surprise attacks or for repelling immediate attacks by others, biological weapons are too slow

---

[16] Certain biological weapons have been developed to target food crops, with the aim of eliminating the enemy's food supply. In addition spore-forming organisms such as anthrax might require major decontamination efforts, which would interfere with normal economic or military activities.

and unpredictable to be militarily attractive. He argues, however, that they might be useful on the front lines against fixed defensive positions in long wars of attrition.[17] Another analyst argues that suitable targets for biological weapons might include reserve combat units, formations massing for an offensive, air force squadrons, and rear area support units. In such cases, even if not many troops were killed, a sudden epidemic of incapacitating disease could temporarily paralyze both logistic and fighting units.

The role of the use, or threat of use, of weapons of mass destruction to create terror makes it difficult to assess what might constitute a "rational" or "irrational" planned use by proliferant states. When leaders threaten to use weapons of mass destruction, whether in an initial or a retaliatory attack, they must decide what level of devastation will be sufficiently intimidating to achieve their purpose. A leader considering a strategic attack with such weapons must not merely calculate the physical effects of the weapons on the other side's war machine, but also subjectively predict the psychological impact of the attack on the other side's population and government. The attacker must also estimate what kind of retaliation to expect, and what he (or his country) would be willing to accept.

Past Uses of Nuclear, Chemical, and Biological Weapons

Nuclear weapons have been detonated on adversaries only twice—on Hiroshima and Nagasaki. According to some estimates, the immediate casualties of the first atomic bomb were 68,000 dead and another 76,000 injured, while those of the second bomb, at Nagasaki, were 8,000 dead and 21,000 injured.[18] Estimates of bomb-related deaths through 1950 are much higher, however: 200,000 in Hiroshima, 140,000 in Nagasaki.[19]

As noted earlier, the United States and the Soviet Union used nuclear weapons during the Cold War to back threats relating to the use of conventional military force. In addition, during the 1962 Cuban Mis-

---

[17] Raymond A. Zilinskas, "Biological Warfare and the Third World," *Politics and the Life Sciences*, Vol. 9, No. 1 (August 1990), pp. 59–76.

[18] Samuel Glasstone and Philip J. Dolan, eds. *The Effect of Nuclear Weapons* (Washington, D.C.: US Departments of Defense and Energy, 1977).

[19] Richard Rhodes, *The Making of the Atomic Bomb*, (New York: Simon and Schuster, 1986).

sile Crisis, the two nations came frighteningly close to nuclear war over the US demand that the USSR withdraw nuclear missiles from Cuba.

According to one analyst, US presidents have used nuclear weapons more than 20 times in efforts to intimidate or coerce opponents in crises and wars in Indochina, East Asia, Berlin, and the Middle East. In such situations, nuclear weapons were "used" in the way a gun is used when it is pointed at someone's head in a confrontation, even if only in a bluff. Some of these threats (many of which were concealed, then and later, from the US public) were regarded by the presidents and their advisers as having been successful in helping to produce the outcomes they sought. Others were not regarded as successful. Most if not all such threats were ambiguous to some degree. At least some of the threats were certainly regarded by the presidents as bluffs; but in no case did that mean there was no danger of escalation.

On various occasions the Soviet Union, Israel, India, and Pakistan have, similarly, employed nuclear weapons in deterrent threats. In the Gulf War, for example, not one of the militarily involved nuclear states explicitly ruled out the use of its nuclear arsenal. In public questioning, US and other officials pointedly refused to exclude the possible first use of their nuclear weapons against Iraq, particularly if Iraq used chemical weapons extensively, which was considered likely.[20]

During World War I, both sides used large amounts of chemical weapons. Egypt reportedly used chemical weapons in Yemen in 1967–1968. Iraq used chemical weapons during the 1980–1988 war with Iran, causing some 50,000 Iranian casualties; and Iran later retaliated in kind. The Iraqi government has also used chemical weapons against Iraq's Kurdish population.

Biological weapons have not played a prominent role in wartime. Japan used biological weapons against China in World War II. The Japanese Army dropped bombs carrying plague-infested fleas on at least 11 Chinese cities. The weapons were not reliable and had little military impact. They claimed an estimated 700 Chinese civilian lives; but contamination of Chinese territory with plague also caused thousands of unintended casualties among Japanese troops.

---

[20] Daniel Ellsberg, "Manhattan Project II: To End the Threat of Nuclear War," *Harvard Journal of World Affairs*, Summer 1992.

Chapter 3

Acquiring Weapons of Mass Destruction

Acquiring Nuclear Weapons

A nuclear weapon is a device that releases large amounts of explosive energy through extremely rapidly occurring nuclear reactions. For a nuclear weapon to work, a minimum "critical mass" of nuclear materials must be present, and that material must be brought together with sufficient speed and precision for a nuclear reaction to be sustained.

Nuclear reactions can be of two types: fission or fusion. Nuclear fission reactions occur when a heavy atomic nucleus is split into two or more smaller nuclei, usually as the result of a bombarding neutron but sometimes occurring spontaneously; fusion occurs when lightweight nuclei are joined, typically under conditions of extreme temperature and pressure. Nuclear weapons utilize either fission or a combination of fission and fusion.

The nuclear material used in a nuclear weapon may be either uranium or plutonium. Uranium occurs naturally in uranium ore. Uranium ore is made up of two isotopes: uranium-235, which readily undergoes the fission process needed in a nuclear weapon, and uranium-238, which does not. Thus, U-235 is termed "fissile" and U-238 is termed "nonfissile." Only about 0.7 percent of uranium in ore is U-235, while 99.3 percent is U-238. To obtain the U-235 needed for nuclear weapons from naturally occurring uranium, the proportion of U-235 to U-238 must be increased, a process called "enrichment."

Uranium-fueled commercial nuclear power reactors use either natural uranium or low-enriched uranium (LEU) with a U-235 content generally in the range of 2 to 5 percent. Over 100 of the approximately 325 research and test reactors worldwide are fueled with highly enriched uranium (HEU), consisting of more than 20 percent U-235. Enrichments above 90 percent are typically used for nuclear weapons. A proliferant state seeking to enrich uranium for nuclear weapons can get a head start by obtaining low-enriched or highly enriched uranium prepared for nuclear power reactors, rather than natural uranium with its lower U-235 content.

Plutonium is a man-made element that has several isotopes. The isotope Pu-239 is fissile; like U-235, it undergoes fission rapidly and thus can be used as the fuel for a nuclear weapon. Plutonium is produced in power reactors as a byproduct of the exposure of the U-238 in fuel elements to neutrons during normal reactor operation. Reactor-grade plutonium, which contains at least 20 percent of the nonfissile isotopes Pu-240 and Pu-242, is produced when fuel elements are exposed to neutrons for long periods of time, typically one to several years. Weapon-grade plutonium typically contains 6 percent or less of the isotopes Pu-240 and Pu-242 that make design of nuclear weapons more difficult. Weapon-grade plutonium is created when U-238 is irradiated in a nuclear reactor for only a short period of time. Plutonium-239 can be used in nuclear weapons after it is separated from the unconverted uranium and other irradiation byproducts in the spent fuel elements by chemical reprocessing; it is then called "separated plutonium." Four major reprocessing facilities, in France, Britain and Russia, can process another country's spent reactor fuel into plutonium for use in its plutonium-based reactors.

Uranium-233, which can be produced in reactors fueled by thorium-232, can also be used to construct a nuclear weapon.

The minimum mass of fissile material that can sustain a nuclear chain reaction, called a "critical mass," depends on the density, shape, and type of fissile material, as well as the effectiveness of any surrounding material (called a reflector or tamper), designed to reflect neutrons back into the fissioning mass.

The two basic designs used to assemble a critical mass of fissile material involve gun-assembly and implosion. In the gun-assembly technique, a propellant charge propels two or more subcritical masses into each other, forming a single supercritical mass inside a high-strength gun-barrel-like container. Compared with the implosion approach, this method assembles the masses relatively slowly and at normal densities; it is practical only with HEU. In the implosion technique, which operates much more rapidly, a shell of chemical high-explosive surrounding the nuclear material is detonated at multiple points simultaneously to rapidly and uniformly compress the nuclear material to form a supercritical mass. The implosion technique requires substantially less nuclear material than the gun-assembly method.

In both types of design, a surrounding tamper may help keep the nuclear material assembled for a longer time before the chain reaction blows apart, thus increasing the yield. The tamper often doubles as a neutron reflector. In a fission weapon, the timing of the initiation of the chain reaction must be carefully controlled for the weapon to have a predictable yield. A neutron generator emits a burst of neutrons to initiate the chain reaction at the proper moment—near the point of maximum compression in an implosion design or of full assembly in the gun-barrel design.[1]

Fusion (or "thermonuclear") weapons derive some of their total energy from fusion reactions, but are commonly triggered by a "primary" fission explosion. The intense temperatures and pressures generated by the fission explosion overcome the strong electrical repulsion that would otherwise keep the positively charged nuclei of the fusion fuel from fusing. In general, the x-rays from the primary fission device heat and compress material surrounding a secondary fusion device. The secondary device usually contains solid lithium-6 deuteride. Such bombs, in theory, can be designed with arbitrarily large yields: the Soviet Union once tested a device with a yield equivalent to about 59 million tons of high explosives.

OBTAINING NUCLEAR WEAPONS FROM THE
FORMER SOVIET UNION

The collapse of the Soviet Union has raised serious concerns over the security of nuclear weapons from theft or sale for the first time since 1945. By mid-1992, according to Russian officials and CIA Director R. James Woolsey, all tactical nuclear weapons had been returned to Russia from the other former Soviet republics. However, since the political situation in Russia itself is unsettled, this move alone does not resolve questions concerning the weapons' security. Moreover, strategic weapons— the higher yield, bulkier weapons designed for intercontinental missile

---

[1]At a presentation at the South African Embassy, Washington, D.C., on July 23, 1993, Waldo Stumpf, chief executive officer of the Atomic Energy Corporation of South Africa, Ltd., stated that South Africa designed a gun-type weapon using HEU that employed no neutron initiator.

Figure 5: Technical Routes to a Nuclear Weapon Capability

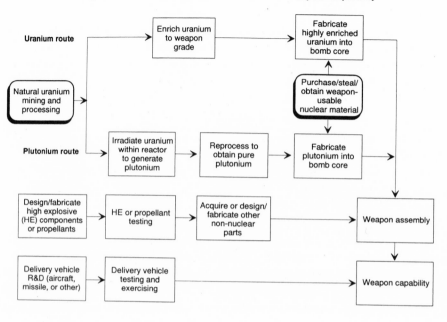

or bomber delivery—are still present in Ukraine, Belarus, and Kazakhstan.

However, even if whole nuclear weapons were transferred to a nonweapon state, it is unlikely in most circumstances that they could be detonated in their present form. All strategic and many tactical weapons in the former Soviet Union are believed to be configured with "permissive action links" (PALs) or equivalent controls that preclude their direct detonation except upon introduction of a special code. However, the level of sophistication of Soviet PALs is not known, and many—especially early models—may be comparatively rudimentary, not integral to the weapon, or entirely absent. Such devices cannot be presumed to delay indefinitely a technically sophisticated individual or team that had prolonged access to the weapon.

Moreover, a smuggled weapon would constitute a serious danger even if it could not be detonated. First, disassembly by suitably trained individuals could provide valuable first-hand information on its design, materials, and components. Second, the weapon's nuclear materials might be recovered for use in another weapon. As such, transfer of any warhead to any nonweapon state would be cause for serious concern, even if its immediate utility as a detonable device were low.

STEPS INVOLVED IN MAKING NUCLEAR WEAPONS

The process for manufacturing nuclear weapons, shown schematically in Figure 5, is complex and difficult. It involves three basic stages. The first, and most difficult, is the production of the special nuclear material—separated plutonium or HEU—that is required in a nuclear warhead.

Second, additional components must be added to make the HEU or separated plutonium into a weapon: chemical explosives (or in the case of gun-type weapons, propellants) to compress the nuclear material into a supercritical mass that will sustain an explosive chain reaction; non-fissile materials to reflect neutrons and tamp the explosion; electronics to trigger the explosives; a neutron generator to start the nuclear detonation (chain reaction) at the desired moment; and associated command, control, and security circuitry. Testing of the nuclear chain reaction process is not necessary, but testing of the non-nuclear chemical explosive system in implosion weapons is required, and tests are used to assess and fine-tune yield estimates. A gun-type weapon made with HEU does not even require chemical-explosive testing. Nuclear explosive testing would be much more important for a proliferant seeking to develop either very low-weight weapons, such as for delivery by missiles of limited payload, or thermonuclear weapons.

The final stage in building a nuclear weapon is to integrate the weapon with a delivery system. Many of the potential proliferants seem to be developing ballistic missiles, and all of them already have combat aircraft. Making nuclear weapons for these delivery systems can be challenging; the weapons must be small and light. However, high-tech military systems are not required to deliver nuclear weapons; other military or civilian vehicles could also be used to deliver larger, less sophisticated nuclear devices.

OBTAINING FISSILE MATERIAL THROUGH DIVERSION OR THEFT

Obtaining fissile material (enriched uranium or plutonium) remains the greatest single obstacle most countries face in attempting to acquire nuclear weapons.

A potential proliferant can acquire fissile material by purchase or theft from another country, by diversion from civilian nuclear activities in violation of IAEA safeguards, or by indigenous production in unsafeguarded facilities. Each of these routes is prohibited to non-nuclear weapon states that are party to the NPT, and to states that are parties to nuclear-weapon-free-zone treaties such as the Treaty of Tlatelolco. Any unsafeguarded facilities that such states did operate would presumably be run covertly. Non-NPT states such as Israel, India, and Pakistan are under no treaty obligations to refrain from acquiring, producing, or selling fissile material or to place all their nuclear production facilities under IAEA safeguards.

Nuclear materials, some of which are relatively easy to convert into forms directly usable in nuclear weapons, are stored at and transported among hundreds of civilian nuclear facilities around the world. These stockpiles and transfers inevitably introduce some risk of theft or diversion. Obviously, theft of weapon-grade nuclear material would be more serious than that of material requiring substantial additional processing. If a particular stockpile were poorly safeguarded, diversion of material might not be detected before it had been fabricated into a weapon. Clandestine diversion probably constitutes a greater danger than the hijacking of a shipment, which would be noticed and might trigger military or other action to recover the stolen material or prevent its use.

Due in part to IAEA safeguards, individual commercial power reactors are neither the most vulnerable nor the most fruitful sites for diverting nuclear materials.

Material might be found at civil nuclear facilities in Russia, or from mothballed facilities in other republics. As an NPT nuclear weapon state, Russia is not subject to mandatory safeguards at any of its nuclear facilities.

To control the HEU from dismantled Russian weapons, the United States has negotiated the purchase of 500 metric tons over the next 20 years for use in US-based commercial power reactors. (The material is to be blended down to LEU in Russia before being transferred.) No comparable purchases are envisioned for weapon-grade plutonium. Thus, Russia may choose to recycle its excess plutonium in its own power reactors or to keep as many as 10,000 to 20,000 plutonium pits (the nuclear weapon cores that contain the fissile material) in long-term storage. Unless adequate measures are taken to regulate their transport, storage, and ultimate disposition, both the plutonium and the HEU could conceivably end up in the wrong hands.

Except for the few nuclear weapon states with unsafeguarded plutonium reprocessing facilities (Israel, India, and possibly North Korea), obtaining plutonium for weapon purposes would require its diversion from one of the major reprocessing facilities, or from smaller facilities in other nations, and subsequent illegal transfer to the target country, or diversion from safeguarded facilities within a country after it had received separated plutonium. Such steps would be legally risky and perhaps very costly to attempt in secret, but they remain a possibility.

Although all the HEU used in non-nuclear weapon states' research reactors is obtained from suppliers that require it to be placed under IAEA safeguards, a nation or terrorist group would have little difficulty in recovering the material from fresh fuel if it were seized from storage at a reactor site or in transit. Most research-reactor fuel, however, has been irradiated, making it much more radioactive and difficult to handle. Theft of such fuel, though likely to be regarded as a very serious incident, would be an unlikely means of acquiring a nuclear arsenal, since quantities are limited in any one location and, in most cases, are significantly less than what is needed for a weapon. For these reasons, the proliferation concerns involving diversion or theft of research reactor fuel are limited.

OBTAINING FISSILE MATERIAL THROUGH INDIGENOUS PRODUCTION

The alternative to stealing, diverting, or purchasing weapon-grade nuclear materials is manufacturing them indigenously. Indigenous production of weapon-grade nuclear material requires a large, complex, and expensive set of specialized facilities, which represent the principal "chokepoints" for preventing nuclear proliferation.

Fissile materials can be produced in many different ways (see Appendix Table 2). Under one approach to nuclear material production, large commercial enrichment facilities producing LEU for nuclear power plants could be reconfigured for higher enrichments. A reconfigured facility would have the enrichment capacity to make HEU for tens of weapons annually from the same amount of uranium source material required each year to fuel just one commercial-size nuclear power plant. Furthermore, each such enrichment facility typically supplies fuel for many tens of power reactors annually.

International nonproliferation policies have made it quite difficult to use turn-key imported facilities to produce weapon-grade materials. The NPT prohibits its parties from exporting major nuclear facilities— especially those for uranium enrichment or reprocessing—unless they are placed under IAEA safeguards.

At least ten different technologies are capable of separating the U-235 needed for weapons from the heavier U-238. The different technologies start with uranium hexafluoride gas or other uranium compounds. These technologies include gaseous diffusion and gas centrifuge, electromagnetic processes, and laser processes. The most common enrichment technologies achieve only a low level of enrichment in each pass, or "stage," and thus require many stages set up in sequence.

Many states have studied a number of different approaches, and at least ten non-nuclear weapon states have built pilot plants or production facilities that employ at least one enrichment method. In India, Pakistan, and Iraq, those facilities have not been safeguarded; in Brazil, Argentina, and South Africa, they have only recently been placed under safeguards.

Most of the sensitive technologies and components used for uranium enrichment fall under strict export controls, both in the United States and abroad, and are therefore very difficult to obtain on the open market. Nevertheless, some have escaped these controls, mainly due to lax enforcement and varying regulations among supplier countries.

Export controls have not been instituted for some components of very old technologies, such as electromagnetic isotope separators (EMIS, also known as "calutrons"), and of very new technologies—some of which have still not been developed to a commercial scale by even the most advanced industrialized countries. For example, magnets and beam sources for EMIS and some lasers that could be used for laser isotope-separation techniques have such widespread commercial applications that they have not been controlled.

The proliferation potential of centrifuges has won considerable attention both because of Iraq's pursuit of the technology before the Gulf War, and because of Pakistan's success at building its own modern gas centrifuge plant with the help of blueprints and purchase orders stolen from a Dutch factory.

Aerodynamic methods have higher separation factors than gaseous diffusion, enabling them to reach high enrichments with fewer stages and smaller facilities. With no moving parts other than compressors and pumps, they are operationally less complex than centrifuges or laser processes.

The smallest, most easily hidden enrichment facilities would be based on energy-efficient processes that achieved high levels of enrichment in just a few stages. For example, laser and possibly plasma separation processes would be quite valuable to a proliferant state seeking a covert enrichment facility. However, energy efficiency and high separation per stage are usually correlated with technical complexity, and these advanced techniques will probably remain relatively inaccessible to developing countries for some time.

Although key aspects are proprietary, chemical separation techniques are based on conventional chemical-engineering technology that is available to a great many countries. This enrichment approach could therefore prove difficult to control if the specific processes and materials involved were reproduced by a proliferant state.

A key step in pursuing the plutonium route is obtaining a source of irradiated uranium, either by diverting spent fuel from a safeguarded reactor or by irradiating uranium in a dedicated plutonium-production reactor. Extracting plutonium from spent fuel utilizes chemical processes that have been within the technological grasp of most middle industrial powers for some time.

The combination of a nuclear reactor and a plutonium reprocessing plant offers a potentially simpler route to weapon-usable material than many methods of uranium enrichment. Israel and India operate indigenously built unsafeguarded reactors and reprocessing facilities, and North Korea has built and operated similar facilities that were initially outside of safeguards.

OBTAINING THE EXPERTISE TO DESIGN AND BUILD A NUCLEAR WEAPON

Although successfully designing a nuclear explosive device requires individuals with expertise in metallurgy, chemistry, physics, electronics, and explosives, the required technology dates back to the 1940s, and the basic physical concepts have been widely known for some time. Much of the relevant physics for a workable design is available in published sources. As Iraq and other nations have discovered, many unclassified or declassified documents make designing a weapon today considerably easier than it was for the first nuclear powers. The first gun-type weapon ever designed, the Hiroshima weapon, was based on such a sure-fire technique that no nuclear test was deemed necessary before it was used in warfare. Nevertheless, knowledge must be supplemented by industrial infrastructure and the resources to carry a nuclear weapon program to completion. Similarly, the technologies for building cars and propeller-driven airplanes date back to early in this century, but many countries still cannot build them indigenously.

Weapon fabrication would probably not present major technical hurdles to a proliferant. Assembly of a gun-type weapon is relatively straightforward. Implosion-designs would require lathes, other machine tools, and possibly isostatic presses to fabricate explosive lenses and other components, but there may be several suppliers of these dual-use items and various ways to import them. Little of the equipment for final assembly of a weapon is sufficiently specialized to be easily controllable by export laws. However, "weaponizing" a nuclear warhead for reliable missile delivery or long shelf life creates hurdles that could significantly increase the required development effort.

The infrastructure and experience gained from civilian nuclear research and nuclear power programs would be of substantial benefit to a nuclear weapon program. Up to a certain point in developing a civilian nuclear fuel cycle, its technology is virtually identical to that used for producing fissile materials for weapons. Relevant experience would include the ability to handle radioactive materials, familiarity with chemical processes for fuel fabrication and with materials having specific chemical or nuclear properties, and the design and operation of reactors and electronic control systems. Although this kind of experience is not unique to the operation of reactors—and is neither necessary nor sufficient to produce a weapon—it would provide a technology base upon which a nuclear weapon program could draw. Furthermore, the infrastructure supporting nuclear power generation and its associated fuel cycle can provide cover for elements of a covert weapon program, even in a country subject to IAEA safeguards.

The principles of nuclear weapons can be discovered without any prior design experience by any competent group of theoretical and experimental physicists and engineers. Although the specifics of designing, analyzing, testing, and producing a nuclear explosive device are certainly not taught in graduate schools, nuclear engineering and physics curricula inevitably provide a basic foundation for work in the area of nuclear weapon design. Indeed, students from many countries each year go abroad for instruction in such fields at top universities. Nevertheless, the assistance of outside experts with specific knowledge of nuclear design can significantly accelerate a program by avoiding "dead-ends" that could waste valuable time and resources.

According to the US State Department, dozens of key Russian scientists would likely be able to direct critical aspects of a weapon program in a developing country, and perhaps 1,000 or 2,000 technicians possess highly useful technical skills. Several dozen nuclear scientists from the former Soviet Union (though probably not weapon designers) have reportedly been working in Iran, with dozens more entering other Middle Eastern countries. Russian and Western specialists, however, say that so far they have no hard evidence that any attempt at recruiting actual nuclear weapon designers has been successful.

In any case, the expertise needed to produce weapon-usable material *and* to make it into a deliverable weapon spans a wide range of disciplines and requires the right mix of individuals. Recruiting any given nuclear weapon specialist could have significant or only marginal utility; this would depend strongly on the particular needs of a country at the time.

Acquiring Chemical Weapons

Although hundreds of thousands of toxic chemicals have been examined over the years for their military potential, only about 60 have been used in warfare or stockpiled in quantity as chemical weapons. Physical properties required of chemical weapon agents include high toxicity, volatility or persistence (depending on the military mission), and stability during storage and dissemination. Lethal agents that have been produced and stockpiled in the past include vesicants such as sulfur mustard and lewisite, which burn and blister the skin, eyes, respiratory tract, and lungs; choking agents such as phosgene and chlorine, which irritate the eyes and respiratory tract; blood agents such as hydrogen cyanide, which starve the tissues of oxygen; and nerve agents such as sarin and VX, which interfere with the transmission of nerve impulses, causing convulsions and death by respiratory paralysis.

Unlike nuclear weapons, which require a large, specialized, and costly scientific-industrial base, chemical weapon agents can be made with commercial equipment generally available to any country. Indeed, few military technologies have evolved as *little* as chemical weapons over the past half-century.

Current-generation mustard and nerve agents are based on scientific discoveries made during and between the two World Wars, and there have been few major innovations since then in either basic chemicals or manufacturing methods. The vast majority of the US stockpile (in terms of tonnage) was produced during the 1950s and 1960s, when the United States managed to produce high-quality chemical weapon agents. Moreover, production techniques for the major chemical weapon agents have been published in the open patent or chemical literature, including data on reaction kinetics, catalysts, and operating parameters. According to analyst Kyle Olson, "The routes of production are generally known, and they can be pursued with relatively primitive equipment, especially by those who are not overly concerned with worker health and safety or environmental impacts."

As the commercial chemical industry has spread around the world in response to the urgent needs of developing countries for chemical fertilizers, pesticides, and pharmaceuticals, the availability of chemicals and equipment required to produce chemical weapon agents has increased. At the same time, thousands of applied organic chemists and chemical engineers from developing countries have been trained in related production technologies at universities in the United States, Europe, and the former Soviet Union.

Chemical weapon agent production is only one step on the path to acquiring a full capability to wage chemical warfare. A supertoxic agent, despite its lethality, does not become a usable weapon until it has been integrated with some form of munition or delivery system.

CHEMICAL WEAPON AGENT PRODUCTION PROCESSES

Some agents (e.g., sulfur mustard and the nerve agent tabun) could be produced with widely available chemical industry equipment; some, such as mustard gas (sulfur mustard), are very simple to produce. During World War I, thousands of tons of mustard gas were produced from alcohol, bleaching powder, and sodium sulfite. During World War II, the two largest producers of mustard gas, the United States and the Soviet Union, used two common industrial chemicals—sulfur monochloride and ethylene—as starting materials. A mustard-gas plant based on this method could be located at an oil refinery, which is an excellent source of ethylene and could also extract the necessary sulfur from petroleum or natural gas.

Today, the precursor of choice for any large-scale production of mustard gas is thiodiglycol, a sulfur-containing organic solvent that has commercial applications in the production of ballpoint pen inks, lubricant additives, plastics, and photographic developing solutions, and as a carrier for dyes in the textile industry. Thiodiglycol is just one chemical step away from sulfur mustard, requiring only a reaction with a chlorinating agent like hydrochloric acid (HCl), a widely available industrial chemical. This process does not require a particularly sophisticated chemical industry; indeed, it could be performed in a basement laboratory with the necessary safety precautions.

When Iraq began mustard-gas production in the early 1980s, it was unable to make thiodiglycol indigenously and ordered more than 1,000 tons from foreign sources. In response to the subsequently threatened embargo on exports of thiodiglycol from Western countries, however, Iraq developed an indigenous production capability based on reacting ethylene oxide with hydrogen sulfide. Both of these ingredients are widely available.

Nerve agents are supertoxic compounds that produce convulsions and rapid death by inactivating an enzyme (acetylcholinesterase) that is essential for the normal transmission of nerve impulses. The nerve agents belong to the class of organophosphorus chemicals, which contain a phosphorus atom surrounded by four chemical groups, one of which is a double-bonded oxygen. In general, nerve agents are 100 to 1,000 times more poisonous than organophosphorus pesticides. The difference in toxicity between nerve agents and pesticides derives from the nature of the chemical groups surrounding the phosphorus atom.

Synthesis of nerve agents includes some difficult process steps involving highly corrosive or reactive materials. These steps are probably more of a nuisance than a true obstacle to a determined proliferant.

Production of the nerve agent tabun is relatively easy. Tabun is made from four precursor chemicals: phosphorus oxychloride ($POCl_3$), sodium cyanide, dimethylamine, and ethyl alcohol, most of which are widely available. Ethanol and sodium cyanide are manufactured and sold in vast quantities; dimethylamine and phosphorus oxychloride are produced by companies in several countries for commercial applications in the production of pharmaceuticals, pesticides, missile fuels, and gasoline additives. The major technical difficulty is the cyanation reaction because of the difficulty of containing the toxic hydrogen cyanide gas used as the reagent.

Production of other nerve agents, such as sarin, soman, and VX, is more difficult, because of an alkylation reaction, in which a methyl group ($-CH_3$) or an ethyl group ($-CH_2CH_3$) is added to the central phosphorus to form a P-C bond. This step is less common and is technically difficult, but nevertheless is used in a handful of commercial products such as some pesticides and fire retardants.

If a high-purity agent with a long shelf-life is required, the supertoxic final product must be distilled—an extremely hazardous operation. Distillation is not necessary if a country plans to produce nerve agents for immediate use, rather than for amassing stockpiles.

A sophisticated production facility to make militarily significant quantities of one class of nerve agents might cost $30–50 million, although dispensing with modern waste-handling facilities might cut the cost in half. Some of the equipment needed may have features that indicate that it may be slated for use in a nerve agent facility; these include corrosion-resistant reactors and pipes and special ventilation and waste-handling equipment. However, such special equipment can be dispensed with by relaxing worker safety and environmental standards and by replacing hardware as it corrodes. Moreover, production is easier if a proliferant country is willing to sacrifice a long shelf-life, and produce only low-quality agent for immediate use.

In general, commercial pesticide plants lack the precursor chemicals (materials from which chemical agents are synthesized), equipment, facilities, and safety procedures required for nerve-agent production. Nevertheless, multi-purpose plants capable of manufacturing organophosphorus pesticides or flame retardants could be converted in a matter of weeks or months to the production of nerve agents.

OBTAINING PRECURSOR CHEMICALS FOR CHEMICAL WEAPONS

Developing countries seeking a chemical weapon capability generally cannot manufacture key precursor chemicals and must purchase them from foreign sources. Because of this dependency, Western governments have attempted to slow chemical weapon proliferation by establishing the Australia Group, a committee that coordinates national export-control regulations to restrict the sale of key chemical weapon precursors to suspected proliferants (see Chapter 5). Of course, the export controls coordinated by the Australia Group cannot prevent countries that are outside this body from selling precursor chemicals: indeed, as Western countries have tightened chemical weapon-related controls, exports from developing nations such as India have increased. Of the 54 precursor chemicals whose exports are regulated by the Australia Group countries, Indian companies export about 15, only 4 of which are subject to Indian government export controls.

Furthermore, to the extent that immediate precursors for mustard and nerve agents are controlled by the Australia Group, a proliferant might seek to circumvent such export controls by:

- substituting an uncontrolled precursor chemical for one that is controlled;
- purchasing relatively small amounts of precursor chemicals from multiple sources, instead of obtaining large quantities from a single source;
- producing more obscure chemical weapon agents whose precursors are still available; or
- acquiring an indigenous capability to manufacture precursor chemicals from simpler compounds whose export is not controlled or that are available from domestic sources.

The development of entirely new classes of chemical weapon agents remains a real possibility. In late 1992, a Russian chemist alleged that a military research institute in Moscow had developed a new binary nerve agent more potent than VX; he was subsequently arrested by the Russian Security Service for disclosing state secrets, but the charges were later dropped.

Toxins of biological origin might also be produced in militarily significant quantities with biotechnological techniques. Some toxins are thousands of times more potent than nerve agents, although they also have operational limitations. Toxin genes can be cloned in bacteria to produce kilogram quantities of formerly rare toxins. Moreover, molecular engineering techniques could lead to the development of more stable toxins. Even so, for the foreseeable future, toxin-warfare agents are unlikely to provide dramatic military advantages over existing chemical weapons.

FROM CHEMICAL WEAPON AGENTS TO CHEMICAL WEAPONS

Agent production is several steps removed from an operational chemical weapon capability, which requires design and development of effective munitions, filling the munitions before use, and mating them with a suitable delivery system. The weaponization of chemical weapon agents involves three steps:

- the use of chemical additives to stabilize or augment the effects of a chemical weapon agent;
- the design and production of munitions for dispersal of the agent; and
- the filling, storage, and transport of munitions.

POTENTIAL DELIVERY SYSTEMS FOR CHEMICAL WEAPONS

In World War I, gaseous agents, such as chlorine and phosgene, were released from ground-based tanks as airborne clouds; later, liquids such as sulfur mustard were delivered in artillery shells. Aerial bombing and spraying methods appeared between the two World Wars. During the Cold War, the United States and the Soviet Union deployed the gamut of chemical delivery systems, from spray tanks to chemical warheads, for short-range ballistic missiles, rockets, land mines, bombs, and artillery.[2] The Iraqi chemical arsenal included artillery shells, bombs, and some ballistic missile warheads.

Acquiring Biological or Toxin Weapon Capability

Biological and toxin warfare (BTW) has been termed "public health in reverse" because it involves the deliberate use of disease and natural poisons to incapacitate or kill people. Potential BTW agents include living microorganisms such as bacteria, rickettsiae, fungi, and viruses that cause infection resulting in incapacitation or death; and toxins, which are non-living chemicals manufactured by bacteria, fungi, plants, and animals. Microbial pathogens must incubate for 24 hours to 6 weeks between infection and the appearance of symptoms. Toxins, in contrast, do not reproduce within the host; they act relatively quickly, causing incapacitation or death within several minutes or hours.

Because of the ability of pathogenic microorganisms to multiply rapidly within the host, small quantities of a biological agent widely disseminated through the air could inflict casualties over a very large area. Weight-for-weight, BTW agents are hundreds to thousands of times more potent than the most lethal chemical-warfare agents, making them true weapons of mass destruction with a potential for lethal mayhem that can exceed that of nuclear weapons.

The technology needed for biological and toxin weapons is information-intensive rather than capital-intensive, and much of the necessary data are available in the published scientific literature. Thus, it is virtually impossible for industrialized states to prevent the diffusion of weapon-relevant information to states of proliferation concern. It has been estimated that more than 100 countries have the capability—if not necessarily the intent—to develop at least crude biological weapons based on standard microbial and toxin agents.

BIOLOGICAL WEAPON AGENTS

Bacteria are single-cell organisms that cause anthrax, brucellosis, tularemia, plague, and numerous other diseases. They vary considerably in infectiousness and lethality. The bacterium that causes tularemia, for example, is highly infectious. Inhalation of as few as ten organisms

---

[2] Chemical agents are most efficiently delivered as a spray at low altitudes.

causes disease after an incubation period of three to five days; if not treated, tularemia results in deep-seated pneumonia from which 30 to 60 percent of victims die within 30 days. Brucellosis, another bacterial disease, has a low mortality rate—about 2 percent—but an enormous capacity to inflict casualties. Infection gives rise to fever and chills, headache, loss of appetite, mental depression, extreme fatigue, aching joints, and sweating.

The bacterial agent that has received the most attention is anthrax, whose pulmonary form is fatal in more than 90 percent of cases. Under certain environmental conditions, anthrax bacteria will transform themselves into rugged spores that are stable under a wide range of conditions of temperature, pressure, and moisture. One gram of dried anthrax spores contains more than 10^{11} particles; since the lethal dose by inhalation in monkeys is between 10^3 and 10^4 spores, a gram of anthrax theoretically contains some 10 million lethal doses.

Rickettsiae resemble bacteria in form and structure, but are intracellular parasites that can only reproduce inside animal cells. Examples of rickettsial diseases that might be used for biological warfare include typhus, Rocky Mountain spotted fever, Tsutsugamuchi disease, and Q fever.

Viruses are intracellular parasites about 100 times smaller than bacteria. They can infect humans, crops, or domestic animals. Viruses consist of a strand of genetic material (DNA or RNA) surrounded by a protective coat that facilitates transmission from one cell to another. The Venezuelan equine encephalitis (VEE) virus causes a highly infectious disease that incapacitates but rarely kills. In contrast, some hemorrhagic fever viruses, such as Lassa or Ebola fever, are exceedingly virulent, killing 70 out of every 100 victims.

Fungi do not generally cause disease in healthy humans, but fungal diseases are devastating to plants and might be used to destroy staple crops and cause widespread hunger and economic hardship. Plant fungal pathogens include rice blast, cereal rust, and potato blight, which can cause crop losses of 70 to 80 percent.

TOXIN WEAPON AGENTS

Most bacterial toxins, including those associated with cholera, tetanus, diphtheria, and botulism, are large proteins. Botulinal toxin, secreted by the soil bacterium Clostridium botulinum, is the most poisonous substance known. The fatal dose of botulinal toxin by injection or inhalation is about 1 nanogram (billionth of a gram) per kilogram, or about 70 nanograms for an adult male. The toxin is also relatively fast-acting, producing death between one and three days in 80 percent of victims. The UN inspections of Iraq after the Gulf War confirmed that the microbiological research facility at Salman Pak had done development work on botulinum toxin as a potential warfare agent. Nevertheless, attempts to weaponize botulinal toxin have in the past failed to prevent the severe loss of toxicity that accompanies dispersion.

Ricin, a plant toxin derived from castor beans, irreversibly blocks cellular protein synthesis. Inhalation of about 10 micrograms (millionths of a gram) is lethal. Castor beans are widely cultivated as a source of castor oil, which has numerous legitimate industrial applications. The paste remaining after the oil has been pressed out contains about 5 percent ricin, which can be purified by biochemical means. According to published reports, Iran has acquired 120 tons of castor beans and is allegedly purifying ricin in pharmaceutical plants.

Nonprotein toxins are small organic molecules that often have a complex chemical structure. They include tetrodotoxin (produced by a puffer fish), saxitoxin (made by marine algae known as dinoflagellates, which are taken up and concentrated by clams and mussels), ciguatoxin and microcystin (synthesized by microscopic algae), palytoxin (made by a soft red Hawaiian coral), and batrachotoxin (secreted by poisonous frogs indigenous to western Colombia). Typical characteristics of nonprotein toxins are high toxicity, the absence of antidotes, heat stability (unlike most protein toxins), resistance to other environmental factors, and speedy action. Saxitoxin, for example, produces initial symptoms within 30 seconds after ingestion and can cause labored breathing and paralysis in as little as 12 minutes. There is no known prophylaxis or therapy, and the lethal dose in 50 percent of those exposed may be as low as 50 micrograms, a potency 1,000 times greater than the chemical nerve agent VX.

ACQUIRING A BIOLOGICAL OR TOXIN WEAPON CAPABILITY
Countries seeking a BTW capability are likely to start with the development of standard agents that have been weaponized in the past, such as anthrax, tularemia, and botulinum toxin. Nearly all proliferant states lack the sophisticated scientific and technological infrastructure needed to develop novel agents such as exotic viruses, whose military characteristics are poorly understood.

Table 2: Key Production Techniques for BTW Agents

Type of agent	Low-tech production	High-tech production
Bacteria	Batch fermentation, production in animals	Genetically engineered strains, continuous-flow fermentation
Rickettsiae and viruses	Cultivation in eggs, mouse brains, or tissue culture (roller bottles)	Culture in mammalian cells grown on beads, microcarriers, or hollow fibers
Protein toxins	Batch fermentation and purification of a bacterial toxin, or extraction of toxin from a plant or animal source	Cloning of toxin gene in microbial host, extraction
Nonprotein toxins	Extraction from plant or animal source	Cloning of a series of genes, each governing production of one of the enzymes needed to complete a step in the biosynthetic pathway

BTW agents are widely accessible. Pathogenic microorganisms are indigenous to many countries and can be cultured from infected wild animals (e.g., plague in rodents), living domestic animals or infected remains (e.g., Q fever in sheep, anthrax in cattle), soil in endemic areas (which may contain trace amounts of anthrax bacteria and other pathogens), and spoiled food. Certain biological supply houses also ship strains of microbial pathogens to scientists throughout the world.

PRODUCTION TECHNIQUES
Methods for culturing organisms and for inducing spore formation are described in the open scientific literature. Many developing countries have acquired industrial microbiology plants for the production of fermented beverages, vaccines, antibiotics, ethanol (from corn or sugar cane), enzymes, yeast, vitamins, food colors and flavorings, amino acids, and single-cell protein as a supplement for animal feeds. This global expansion of the civilian biotechnology industry, combined with the growing number of molecular biotechnologists trained in the West, has created much broader access to the expertise and equipment needed for the development of BTW agents.

In contrast to chemical-warfare agents, no specialized starting materials are required for the production of biological and toxin agents except for a small seed stock of a disease-producing organism. Nutrients such as fermentation medium, glucose, phosphates, peptone, and a protein source (e.g., casein, electrodialyzed whey, or beef bouillon) are widely available and are routinely imported by developing countries with commercial fermentation industries. Microbial pathogens such as plague bacteria can also be cultivated in living animals, ranging from rats to horses.

Production techniques for the various types of BTW agents are summarized in Table 2. With the advanced fermentation techniques available today, a militarily significant supply of BTW agents could be produced in several days, obviating the need for the long-term stockpiling of agents. As a result, a BTW production facility might remain largely quiescent in peacetime. After completing research and development, weaponization, and pilot-production tests on BTW agents, a proliferant could build production and storage facilities and either keep them mothballed or use them for legitimate commercial purposes.

An industrial fermentation plant suitable for conversion to BTW agent production could be built for about $10 million. In such a "no-frills" facility, bacteria could be grown in standard dairy tanks, brewery fermenters, or even in the fiberglass tanks used by gas stations.

High levels of purity are not required for BTW agents; 60 to 70 percent purity is sufficient and easy to obtain. The main technical hurdles in bacterial production are:

- the danger of infecting production workers;
- genetic mutations that may lead to a loss of agent potency; and
- the contamination of bacterial cultures with other microbes (e.g., bacterial viruses) that may kill them or interfere with their effects.

Pathogenic viruses and rickettsiae, both of which can only reproduce inside living cells, can be cultivated in intact living tissue (such as chick embryos or mouse brains) or in isolated cells growing in tissue culture. The latter approach is technically simpler because it requires only flasks and a nutrient medium. Over the past decade, new methods for cultivating mammalian cells have been developed that permit higher concentrations of cells. The new cell culture techniques greatly simplify the production of viruses and rickettsiae, and allow large-scale yields from very small facilities.

The most efficient way to produce bacterial toxins is through fermentation. Botulinal toxin, for example, is derived from a culture of Clostridium botulinum bacteria, which multiply rapidly under the right conditions of temperature, acidity, and the absence of oxygen. It takes only about three days to grow up a dense culture of the bacterial cells, which extrude botulinal toxin into the surrounding culture medium. A crude preparation of toxin can be freeze-dried down to a solid cake, which can then be milled into a fine powder suitable for dissemination through the air. The milling operation is exceedingly hazardous, however, and must be carried out under strict containment precautions. Plant toxins such as ricin, whose raw material is widely available, could easily be produced in the hundreds of kilograms. With recombinant-DNA techniques, rare animal toxins—formerly available only in milligram amounts—can be prepared in significant quantities in microorganisms. Although these techniques are still largely restricted to the advanced industrial countries, they are spreading rapidly around the world.

Since working with pathogenic microorganisms is extremely hazardous, special physical containment or "barrier" measures are needed to protect plant workers and the surrounding population from infection.

FROM AGENT TO WEAPON

Another challenge is "weaponizing" the BTW agents for successful delivery. Since microbial pathogens and toxins are susceptible to environmental stresses such as heat, oxidation, and desiccation, to be effective they must maintain their potency during weapon storage, delivery, and dissemination.

BTW agents are generally most effective if disseminated within a few days after production. If rapid use is not feasible, the live agents must be converted into a more stable form so that they can survive the stresses of storage, transport, and dissemination. One method for enhancing the stability of BTW agents is rapid freezing and subsequent dehydration under a high vacuum, a process known as freeze-drying. In a few hours, a freeze-drying machine of the type used in the pharmaceutical industry can reduce a solution of bacteria and a sugar stabilizer to a small cake of dried material that can be milled to any degree of fineness. Another approach to stabilization, known as microencapsulation, emulates natural spore formation by coating droplets of pathogens or particles of toxin with a thin coat of gelatin, sodium alginate, cellulose, or some other protective material.

Possible BTW delivery systems range in complexity and effectiveness from an agricultural sprayer mounted on a truck to a specialized cluster warhead carried on a ballistic missile. The difficulty of delivery-system development depends on the proliferant's military objectives. It is not hard to spread BTW agents indiscriminately for the purpose of producing large numbers of casualties over a wide area; it is much more difficult to develop BTW munitions that have predictable or controllable military effects against point targets, such as troop concentrations on a battlefield.

The primary challenge in weaponizing BTW agents for long-range delivery is to keep them alive long enough to infect enemy troops. The agent must be capable of withstanding the physical stresses involved in dissemination without losing its activity.

Acquiring Delivery Systems

Delivery vehicles may be based on very simple or very complex technologies. Under the appropriate circumstances, for instance, trucks, small boats, civil aircraft, larger cargo planes, or ships could be used to deliver or threaten to deliver at least a few weapons to nearby or more distant targets. Any organization that can smuggle large quantities of illegal drugs could probably also deliver weapons of mass destruction using similar means, and the source of the delivery might not be known.

This section focuses on "high end" delivery systems—ballistic missiles, cruise missiles, and combat aircraft—for three reasons. First, simpler systems, such as cars and trucks, boats, civil aircraft, and artillery systems are not amenable to international control. No nonproliferation policy could possibly prevent countries with weapons of mass destruction from delivering them in such vehicles. Second, modern delivery systems enable a country to do more damage to a greater number and variety of targets, with greater reliability, and potentially at longer range, than do low-technology alternatives. Ballistic and cruise missiles in particular may have added psychological effects, since they can be harder to defend against, or even detect, than manned aircraft. Third, as noted in Chapter 2, all but one of the proliferant states has combat aircraft, and most have simple ballistic missiles with a range of 200 to 400 miles. In addition to the declared nuclear powers, an estimated 19 countries have some ballistic missile production capability, and five countries have developed cruise missiles.

COMBAT AIRCRAFT
Combat aircraft with a range of 800 to 1,500 km (500 to 930 miles) are widely available on the open market because most nations with advanced arms industries actively support the efforts of their aerospace companies to make international sales. Over the past several years, trade in advanced combat aircraft has been brisk. During 1983-1992, the 20 developing countries having the largest air forces ordered a total of over 3,800 aircraft.[3] Of those aircraft, over two-thirds were ordered by proliferant nations that either now possess or are thought to be developing weapons of mass destruction, or were thought to be developing them at the time of the orders.

BALLISTIC MISSILES
To deliver weapons at intercontinental range, developing and building intercontinental ballistic missiles may be easier than acquiring long-

---

[3] Jonathan Cohen and Andrew Peach, *IDDS Almanac 1994: World Combat Aircraft Holdings, Production, and Trade* (Cambridge, MA: Institute for Defense and Disarmament Studies, 1994), Tables 1.2 and 1.5.

range bombers and refueling capabilities. In the past, countries have been able to enhance their missile capabilities substantially from what they could have done on their own by importing missiles or advanced components, or by participating in joint ventures (e.g., between Argentina, Egypt, and Iraq to develop the *Condor II* missile). However, since the Missile Control Technology Regime (MTCR) has restricted many of the outside sources of cooperation and assistance on missile development (see Chapter 5), indigenous capability has become more important for most countries that wish to build weapons of mass destruction.

Many countries that already have some ballistic missile production capability could extend that capability in the next ten years. According to at least two estimates, during the next decade South Korea, Brazil, and possibly North Korea and South Africa could join Israel, India, and Taiwan in developing the capability to produce intercontinental-range ballistic missiles. Pakistan, Iran, Argentina, and Egypt could manufacture Scud-range missiles. If countries are willing to dedicate sufficient resources to their missile programs, most of these advances in capability could occur even under a well-functioning MTCR. However, MTCR constraints can significantly increase development costs, helping to convince leaders that the benefits are not worth the expense.

Instead of developing ballistic missiles directly or reverse-engineering short-range missiles, a country might also try to recruit technical personnel from nations with more expertise or attract foreign assistance in developing a space-launch capability.

CRUISE MISSILES

Cruise missiles or other unmanned aerial vehicles that exceed the MTCR thresholds are not widespread outside of the United States and the former Soviet Union, but a number of systems with ranges of 50 to 200 km (30 to 120 miles) are available for purchase.

In the past, indigenous development of guidance and propulsion systems for long-range cruise missiles presented almost insurmountable barriers for developing countries. In recent years, however, near-revolutionary advances in satellite navigation, long-distance communications, composite materials, and light-weight turbojet and turbofan engines have greatly facilitated cruise missile development in a growing number of countries. Furthermore, although the MTCR guidelines have restricted the export of complete systems and dedicated components for systems exceeding the 300 km range, 500 kg payload (190 mile,

1,100 lb.) threshold since 1987, relatively sophisticated ready-made components from unrestricted short-range antiship cruise missiles and unmanned aerial vehicles have been readily available for some time. Trade in these components—many of which have civilian utility—is making the manufacture of longer-range systems considerably easier than in the past.

Israel, Italy, Japan, Sweden, and Taiwan have all developed cruise missiles that can fly far more than 300 km. Brazil, Germany, Iraq, and North Korea also appear to have potential cruise missile programs developing a variety of systems, most of shorter range. In addition, in 1992 Russia exhibited several cruise missile designs that could be developed for export, or even remanufactured by other countries to begin programs of their own.

Chapter 4

Current Treaties and Agreements

To attempt to curb the proliferation and use of weapons of mass destruction, the international community has negotiated three major multilateral treaties that ban the possession of nuclear, chemical, and biological weapons. These agreements, each with more than 130 parties, have codified strong if not yet universal international norms against possessing weapons of mass destruction. Compliance with these treaties is verified by measures of varying rigor. Each pact is ultimately enforced by the UN Security Council, which can call for economic sanctions or military action. (Some nations have created export control regimes to limit the transfer of weapon technology to states of proliferation concern. These controls are discussed in Chapter 5.)

Before a treaty can be implemented, several procedural steps must be completed. First, negotiators need to reach agreement on exactly what language to use in the treaty text; this is usually the most time-consuming step, often taking years or even decades. Once the negotiators agree on the final text, they establish a date for the treaty to be opened for signature by national representatives, which makes their nations signatories. Simply signing a treaty does not create a legal obligation, but international custom calls for signatories to comply with the treaty's principles after they sign. Signatory nations must ratify the treaty according to their national laws, a step that often requires treaty approval by the national legislature. Once a nation ratifies an accord it must submit the instruments of ratification to one of the treaty's depositary nations responsible for tracking treaty membership. A treaty signatory becomes a treaty party once it deposits its instruments of ratification.

Every treaty specifies how many nations, and perhaps which ones, must deposit their instruments of ratification before the treaty enters into force and becomes legally binding, requiring its parties to adhere to the provisions of the agreement. Nations wishing to join a treaty after it enters into force must first ratify the agreement, and then deposit their instruments of accession with a depositary nation; they are immediately bound to implement the treaty.

Multilateral Nuclear Weapon Treaties

NUCLEAR NONPROLIFERATION TREATY (NPT)

As of January 1, 1995, 167 nations were party to the NPT, including all five declared nuclear weapon states: Britain, China, France, Russia, and the United States. Notable exceptions include three nations generally believed to have nuclear weapons, or the capability to assemble nuclear weapons at short notice: India, Israel, and Pakistan.

The NPT prohibits all member-states except the five acknowledged nuclear powers from acquiring nuclear weapons. It also requires all non-nuclear weapon member-states to implement a safeguards agreement with the International Atomic Energy Agency (IAEA) covering all nuclear materials that might be useful for weapons. IAEA safeguards are intended to detect and deter the diversion of materials from peaceful nuclear programs to military use.

Under the NPT, non-nuclear weapon parties must declare to the IAEA all facilities that handle nuclear materials, and these facilities then become subject to safeguards. But the IAEA has had little ability to monitor whether states were conducting nuclear weapon activities in *undeclared* facilities. The limitations of this approach became clear after the 1991 Gulf War, when Iraq was revealed to have mounted a major nuclear weapon program out its declared facilities. Although monitoring declared nuclear facilities will continue to be crucial to verifying compliance with the NPT, it addresses only half the problem. Some means must also be found to allay suspicions that nuclear weapon activities might be undertaken in covert or undeclared facilities.

The IAEA has always had the formal ability to undertake "special inspections" of undeclared facilities if it had reason to suspect illicit activities there. However, it did not seek to exercise this authority until February 1993, when it attempted to inspect suspicious sites in North Korea. (In response, North Korea refused access to IAEA inspectors and, in March 1993, announced its withdrawal from the NPT. Later, under an October 1994 agreement, North Korea promised to allow all IAEA inspections, including the special inspection, of two nuclear reactors, once they are constructed in North Korea by a US-organized consortium of nations (see Chapter 2). In the meantime, North Korea has agreed to suspend all of its nuclear activities, and has agreed to allow the IAEA to verify this freeze.) To carry out inspections of undeclared sites, the IAEA must be able to receive and act on information identifying suspect facilities, and it must have the backing of the UN Security Council in case the target state refuses to cooperate. To date, the IAEA has only reported two violations (Iraq and North Korea), and in neither case did the Security Council impose economic sanctions or call for military action.

Since the NPT entered into force in 1970 for a 25-year period, a review conference is being held in 1995 at which member-states must decide whether to extend the treaty, and for how long. Consequently, successful extension of the NPT is one of the most important issues facing the nuclear nonproliferation regime (see Chapter 6).[1]

TREATIES OF TLATELOLCO AND RAROTONGA

As of January 1, 1995, all but three Latin American and Caribbean nations have brought the Treaty of Tlatelolco into force. The three exceptions are Cuba, St. Kitts and Nevis, and St. Lucia. Eleven South Pacific nations, including Australia and New Zealand, are party to the Treaty of Rarotonga.

Parties to the Treaty of Tlatelolco agree not to acquire or to permit the presence on their territory of nuclear weapons. Similarly, the Treaty of Rarotonga creates a nuclear-free zone in the South Pacific. Both of these nuclear-weapon-free-zone treaties create regional organizations to monitor compliance and also require that member states submit to full-scope IAEA safeguards.

AFRICAN NUCLEAR-WEAPON-FREE ZONE

At the request of the UN General Assembly in 1990, a group of diplomatic experts from African nations began in 1991 to develop a nuclear-weapon-free zone in Africa. The group nearly completed the

---

[1] The NPT review conference was scheduled to begin at UN headquarters in New York on April 17, 1995, shortly after this book went to press.

text of a treaty in 1994 and the treaty is expected to be opened for signature in 1995.

Multilateral Chemical Weapon Treaties

CHEMICAL WEAPON CONVENTION (CWC)

As of January 1, 1995, 159 nations had signed the Chemical Weapon Convention, which opened for signature on January 13, 1993, and 19 had ratified it. The treaty will enter into force 180 days after the 65th signatory formally submits its instruments of ratification. Russia and the United States, owners of the two largest chemical weapon stockpiles, have signed the treaty but have not yet ratified it.

The Chemical Weapon Convention bans the development, production, possession, and use of chemical weapons and establishes the most comprehensive verification scheme yet formulated in an international treaty. When it comes into force, it will create a new international institution—the Organization for the Prohibition of Chemical Weapons (OPCW)—that will receive routine declarations from member states and conduct routine inspections of declared chemical facilities. More important, it will have the ability to conduct "challenge inspections" at any site—government or private—suspected of illegal activity.

Far more facilities produce, ship, or use chemicals than are involved in peaceful nuclear activities, making the routine notification and inspection activities of the OPCW much more complicated than those of the IAEA. Moreover, the CWC's challenge inspection provisions are much more rigorous than the IAEA's provisions for "special inspections." The final treaty text—and the implementation procedures now being negotiated among treaty signatories—are based on the principal of "managed access," in which the state being searched has the right to limit the access of treaty inspectors in order to protect information not germane to the treaty. An important hurdle in implementing the CWC's inspection provisions will be balancing the need to monitor treaty compliance with the need to protect proprietary and national-security information unrelated to the CWC.[2]

---

[2] See Office of Technology Assessment, *The Chemical Weapons Convention: Effects on the US Chemical Industry*, OTA-BP-ISC-106 (Washington, D.C., US Government Printing Office, August 1993).

GENEVA PROTOCOL OF 1925
As of January 1, 1994, 130 nations were party to the Geneva Protocol of 1925. The parties agree not to use "asphyxiating, poisonous, or other gases" or "bacteriological methods" in warfare. The United States ratified the Protocol in 1975, at that time reserving the right to retaliate with chemical weapons against states not observing the Protocol; it has rescinded that reservation, effective with signing the CWC in January 1993. The protocol has no verification or enforcement provisions.

Multilateral Biological Weapon Treaties

BIOLOGICAL WEAPON CONVENTION (BWC)
As of January 1, 1995, 134 nations were party to the Biological Weapon Convention. Signed in 1972, the convention bans development, production, and stockpiling of biological agents or toxins for purposes other than "prophylactic, defensive, and other peaceful activities." Unlike the NPT or the CWC, however, it makes no explicit provisions for verification. The treaty text requires only that member states are to "consult one another" and "cooperate in solving any problems which may arise in relation to the objective" of the treaty. States believing other states to be in breach of the treaty may lodge a complaint with the UN Security Council, and states are obligated to cooperate with any Security Council investigation. The Biological Weapons Convention became effective in 1975.

Pursuant to the Third Review Conference of the BWC in 1991, an expert working group has been considering means by which a verification regime for the BWC might be instituted. Balancing the degree of intrusiveness needed to detect or deter cheating with the need to protect proprietary and national-security information will be even more difficult for the BWC than it is for the CWC.

Under the Bush administration, the United States opposed implementation of a verification regime on the grounds that development and production of biological weapons—much more so than chemical or nuclear weapons—are easy to hide. Therefore, a formal verification regime would not prove to be much of a deterrent to cheating, nor would it provide sufficient confidence in other states' compliance to be worth the costs of conducting and submitting to highly intrusive inspections. Moreover, the United States argued that ineffective verification measures could instill a false sense of confidence and prove to be worse than no verification regime at all.

Other states, including many US allies, countered that even a modest verification regime has some prospect of catching violations and that any state contemplating cheating would have to take that risk into account. Moreover, the verification regime would mandate declarations of all activities relevant to the Biological Weapons Convention. These declarations, when combined with on-site inspections, would make it easier to detect anomalies indicative of a violation.

Under the Clinton administration, the United States altered its policy and supported new measures to share more information among BWC parties to increase confidence that parties were in compliance with the treaty.

In September 1993, the UN expert group released a list of compliance measures that treaty parties could adopt, and the treaty parties established an ad hoc group in September 1994 began drafting a legally binding compliance regime using some or all of the suggested measures.

Other Agreements on Nuclear, Chemical and Biological Arms

In addition to joining multilateral agreements, some nations have implemented bilateral or few-party pacts to limit or ban the possession of weapons of mass destruction.

NUCLEAR WEAPONS

Most notably, Belarus, Kazakhstan, Russia, Ukraine, and the United States have begun to implement the Strategic Arms Reduction Treaty (START) by dismantling nuclear warheads and their delivery vehicles. Under START, the United States and the Soviet Union agreed to reduce their stockpiles to 1,600 strategic nuclear delivery vehicles carrying no more than 6,000 warheads as counted by the treaty (actual numbers could be much higher). In 1992, Belarus, Kazakhstan, and Ukraine agreed that Russia would be the only former Soviet state to retain nuclear weapons. In addition, Russia and the United States may soon ratify START II, which will lower the number of deployed strategic nuclear weapons to 3,000–3,500 for each side by 2003. To help the former Soviet states implement the START agreements, the United

States and other Western nations are providing financial assistance for nuclear weapon destruction projects in the former Soviet Union.

To end the development of new nuclear weapons, both Russia and the United States have continued a moratorium on nuclear testing declared by the Soviet Union in 1991 and joined by the United States in 1992. Furthermore, the United States has ended production of new nuclear weapons and Russia has indicated that it will do likewise.

Other nations have also reached bilateral nuclear agreements, including North and South Korea and Argentina and Brazil. The two Koreas signed a denuclearization agreement in December 1991, promising not to develop, produce, possess, or use nuclear weapons. Implementation of this agreement was suspended when North Korea announced its intent to withdraw from the NPT in March 1993. Argentina and Brazil signed the Iguazu Falls Agreement in 1990, agreeing to ban possession of nuclear weapons. The agreement created a bilateral agency to conduct inspections and initiated IAEA inspections.

CHEMICAL WEAPONS

Before the multilateral Chemical Weapon Convention was completed, the Soviet Union and the United States signed the 1989 Wyoming Joint Memorandum, which provides for a bilateral exchange of information on chemical weapon stockpiles, and the 1990 Bilateral Destruction Agreement, requiring the destruction of most of the Soviet and US stockpiles within ten years. Russia has assumed the Soviet obligations under the two agreements, but implementation has proceeded slowly as the United States has questioned the Russian declarations and Russia has asked for modifications to this agreement.

BIOLOGICAL WEAPONS

To resolve concerns over compliance with the BWC, Britain, Russia, and the United States reached a trilateral accord in September 1992 to allow visits to each other's facilities. These visits began in late 1992 and continued through 1994, but the three sides have continued to express concerns about compliance with the treaty.

Chapter 5

Nonproliferation Strategies

Strategies of Prevention

Strategies to prevent proliferation include the indirect approach of improving international security, as well as direct approaches such as export controls, limiting access to knowledge, and threatening proliferants with economic sanctions or military action. This section discusses these strategies.

SECURITY IMPROVEMENTS

Coercive measures by themselves may not always be sufficient to stop states from acquiring weapons of mass destruction. The best hope for nonproliferation in the long term lies in building a consensus among potential proliferants that they should jointly refrain from acquiring these weapons. Unfortunately, such a consensus will be difficult to achieve. States seeking weapons of mass destruction may want them for military purposes (including intimidation or deterrence), for political influence, for national pride, or for international status. The presence of nearby nuclear powers is a powerful and cascading incentive to develop nuclear weapons. (China acquired nuclear weapons because of the United States and the Soviet Union, India because of China, Pakistan because of India, etc.) To forgo weapons of mass destruction, potential proliferants must come to see that their political or military needs can be met in some other way.

EXPORT CONTROLS

Proliferant nations, particularly the less industrialized ones, generally need materials, equipment, and knowledge from abroad to acquire weapons of mass destruction, so blocking their access to such supplies can hinder their progress. This is especially true for nuclear weapons and missiles. Obstacles that can be put in the way of states trying to acquire weapons of mass destruction include restricting the flow of knowledge through secrecy; adopting export controls; taking diplomatic or other action to stop exports by third parties; and acting to stop or discourage experts from providing assistance. To be effective, such measures must be imposed multilaterally.

Export controls are intended to block the most straightforward paths to developing weapons of mass destruction and to increase the costs and time required to pursue alternate approaches. They can also provide information valuable in monitoring programs to develop weapons of mass destruction. Export controls will remain an important component of nonproliferation policy for years, especially in the nuclear area. However, control regimes can be defeated if their targets can invent substitutes for restricted technologies or products, if controls are attempted on goods that are too widely available, or if some potential suppliers are not included. Moreover, it is very difficult to control the education of scientists and engineers in one country who may later return or migrate to another to develop weapons of mass destruction.

In general, manufacturing steps that are particularly time-consuming or difficult for proliferants to master without outside assistance might be exploited to control proliferation. Conversely, steps that are relatively easy, or that make use of widely available know-how and equipment, make poor candidates for control efforts. It is important to understand the extent to which "dual-use" technologies or products—which have legitimate civil applications in addition to their military applications—are involved in the development of weapons of mass destruction; both the feasibility of controlling dual-use items and the implications of doing so depend on the extent of their other applications.

In the United States, export controls are established by a number of public laws and regulations, and they are also formally or informally coordinated with those of other states. They now cover a range of technologies related to nuclear, chemical, and biological weapons, as well as ballistic missiles and conventional armaments.

Export controls have been a major tool of US nonproliferation policy since the Atomic Energy Act of 1946 (superseded by the Atomic Energy Act of 1954, itself amended several times since then). Appendix Table 3 summarizes US laws and regulations directed at restricting US exports (or re-export of US-originated items) that could contribute to the proliferation of weapons of mass destruction or of missiles.

The United States has attempted to enlist other supplier countries in nonproliferation export controls. Appendix Table 4 summarizes the results of these efforts. Three of the groups shown in the table have been organized to control exports. Members of the Nuclear Suppliers Group agree to control their exports of dual-use nuclear technology. Members of the Australia Group agree to control exports of chemical and biological weapon equipment. Members of the Missile Technology Control Regime (MTCR) agree to control exports of missile technology. The overlapping membership of these three groups is shown in Figure 6. Participants in the MTCR refrain from selling ballistic or cruise missiles with ranges over 300 kilometers (190 miles) and payloads greater than 500 kg (1,100 lbs.), or with any range if the seller has reason to believe that they may be used to carry weapons of mass destruction. However, as noted in Chapter 3, missiles with ranges up to 300 km (190 miles)—and to a lesser extent, up to 600–1,000 km (370–620 miles)—are already deployed in many Third World countries.

The United States can impede weapon programs in proliferant states by helping foreign governments block aid that their own citizens or corporations may be providing. If US intelligence uncovers foreign plans to provide such assistance, the United States can request the government having jurisdiction over such activities to stop them. In addition, US laws allow the government to impose sanctions directly against foreign individuals or companies. If a foreign government is aiding proliferation, the United States can take diplomatic measures against it, including the denial of trade preferences, arms transfers, or financial assistance. The purpose of sanctions against suppliers to proliferant nations is primarily deterrence, not revenge; policymakers hope that potential suppliers will not want to risk US sanctions.

Some other supplier nations have legal sanctions comparable to those of the United States.

Other sanctions against suppliers—including nations, not just "persons"—that have been considered by the US Congress have included:

- denial of most-favored nation trade status;
- forfeiture of property and assets;
- denial of assistance from international institutions in which the United States participates;
- denial of arms transfers from the United States;

**Figure 6: Overlapping Membership Among
Nonproliferation Export Control Regimes**

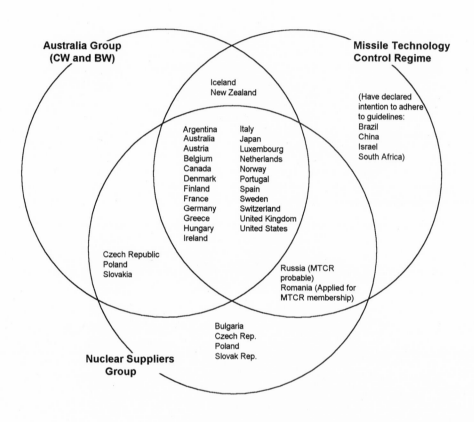

**Australia Group
(CW and BW)**

**Missile Technology
Control Regime**

Iceland
New Zealand

(Have declared
intention to adhere
to guidelines:
Brazil
China
Israel
South Africa)

Argentina	Italy
Australia	Japan
Austria	Luxembourg
Belgium	Netherlands
Canada	Norway
Denmark	Portugal
Finland	Spain
France	Sweden
Germany	Switzerland
Greece	United Kingdom
Hungary	United States
Ireland	

Czech Republic
Poland
Slovakia

Russia (MTCR
probable)
Romania (Applied for
MTCR membership)

Bulgaria
Czech Rep.
Poland
Slovak Rep.

**Nuclear Suppliers
Group**

- denial of US Export-Import Bank credits;
- termination of co-development and co-production agreements;
- blocking of international financial transactions;
- suspension of aircraft landing rights; and
- prohibition of loading and unloading of cargo from sanctioned countries in US ports.

The president can take several of these actions at his own discretion under his powers to conduct foreign policy.

Tightening export controls and applying sanctions against foreign violators can have economic and political costs. First, controls can somewhat restrict international trade. Although the number of export deals denied is a small fraction of all international transactions, many transactions must be screened in order to detect those that will be denied. Consequently, a wide range of businesses must keep informed about and comply with complex regulations and licensing procedures. Some companies may lose significant legitimate sales and the other business opportunities that might have followed those sales. More seriously for US jobs and exports, US firms may lose market share to foreign competitors that are under less stringent controls. In such cases, not only do the US firms lose business, but other suppliers obviate any nonproliferation benefits that the blockage or delay of sales might have had.

Export controls can also affect international development policy: tighter control of dual-use technologies may hinder weapon proliferation, but it may also stunt the peaceful technological advancement of the importing countries. On the other hand, if controls are targeted to suspected proliferants, countries that cooperate with nonproliferation regimes should not find their peaceful development hindered.

LIMITING ACCESS TO KNOWLEDGE

Export of equipment and blueprints is one way to transfer weapon technologies; export of experts is another. Proliferants may hire foreign experts to work directly on their weapon programs, to advise their own personnel, or to train their own experts. Alternatively, they may send their own scientists and engineers abroad for education and training applicable to weapon programs.

There are several ways that supplier nations can try to control such transfers of expertise. They can enforce secrecy laws that make it illegal for those with classified knowledge to transfer the information. They can also make it illegal to aid or abet proliferants. For example, only since the passage of the Foreign Trade and Payments Act of 1992 have German courts been able to impose prison sentences on German engineers abroad whose activities promote the development or manufacture of nuclear, chemical, or biological weapons. Similarly, the US Atomic Energy Act has long prohibited US nationals from sharing nuclear technology with others.

Another way to restrict the outflow of experts is not to punish, but to reward. For example, Western nations are attempting to establish science and technology centers to employ some of the unemployed and underemployed former Soviet weapon scientists who might otherwise be tempted to emigrate to proliferant countries to work on weapons of mass destruction.

It is much more difficult to limit the education of foreigners in disciplines that could in principle be applied to weapon development. For example, nuclear physics, chemical engineering, and biochemistry may be useful for nuclear, chemical, or biological weapon programs, but they also have fully legitimate civilian applications. Indeed, the NPT, the CWC, and the BWC all stress the obligation of advanced countries to extend peaceful technical training to less developed countries.

Brains are multi-use instruments. To bar foreign nationals from educational institutions on the grounds that they might someday work on weapons would exact a high cost: it would damage the openness in which scholarship thrives, and it would deprive developing countries of legitimate technical advancement.[1] On the other hand, somewhat less draconian policies might be considered. First, governments could record and analyze the subjects of research and study of foreigners to see if suspicious patterns emerge for particular countries. Such a measure might yield additional information about proliferation activities, even if it did not itself serve as a means of control. Second, the citizens of specific countries could be denied educational services if their countries were suspected of developing weapons of mass destruction, or if their countries failed certain criteria, such as joining and adhering to the NPT or the CWC. Such a policy, however, would require putting nonproliferation above other concerns about relations with those countries—it would mean treating those states as international pariahs.

---

[1] Since a significant proportion of US college engineering teachers are of foreign origin, US education might also suffer from such a policy.

ECONOMIC INCENTIVES TO FORGO WEAPONS OF MASS DESTRUCTION

Imposing obstacles to proliferation and threatening to punish potential proliferants are essentially coercive strategies. Another strategy is consensual: offer benefits in exchange for self-restraint. Although unlikely to sway a determined proliferant, financial, technical, and other development assistance can be offered to states forgoing the development of weapons of mass destruction. Instead of serving primarily as an incentive to adopt other nonproliferation policies, development assistance could itself be a nonproliferation measure to the extent that lack of development, economic deprivation, and competition for economic resources are a source of conflict. Similarly, policies that alleviate international tensions resulting from demographic trends, differing political systems, ideology, and resource pressures can also be considered nonproliferation measures.

Linking technical or financial assistance to nonproliferation began with President Eisenhower's 1953 Atoms for Peace Plan. That plan proposed the creation of the IAEA, whose mission would be to make peaceful applications of atomic energy globally available while ensuring that nuclear materials were not diverted to weapons.[2] In the NPT, parties agree to foster peaceful applications of nuclear energy for peaceful purposes, "especially in the territories of non-nuclear weapon States Party to the Treaty, with due consideration for the needs of the developing areas of the world"; they also undertake to ensure that the benefits of peaceful nuclear explosions are available to non-nuclear-weapon states.[3] The US Nuclear Nonproliferation Act of 1978 also links assistance to nonproliferation, while recognizing that in disseminating peaceful applications of nuclear technology, the potential for contributing to weapon applications as well cannot be avoided. The Act provides that the United States "shall seek to cooperate with and aid developing countries in meeting their energy needs through the development of

---

[2] The IAEA is now responsible for inspecting the nuclear facilities of nations that have signed the NPT, and some facilities in non-NPT nations, to ensure that the facilities are not used to make nuclear weapons.

[3] Peaceful nuclear explosions were once a major bone of contention in nonproliferation debates; in principle, there is no difference between a device that could create a peaceful nuclear explosion and one that would create a destructive one. There now appears to be little international political support for maintaining the peaceful nuclear explosion option.

non-nuclear energy resources and the application of non-nuclear technologies" and shall seek to encourage other industrialized nations to do the same.

The BWC calls for parties to facilitate the exchange of equipment, materials, and scientific and technological information for the use of biological agents and toxins for peaceful purposes; parties able to do so are also to cooperate in contributing to the further development and application of scientific discoveries in the field of biology for prevention of disease or for other peaceful purposes.

Article XI of the CWC specifies that its provisions will be carried out "in a manner which avoids hampering the economic or technological development" of parties to the treaty. It also provides that the parties "undertake to facilitate, and have the right to participate in, the fullest possible exchange of chemicals, equipment and scientific and technical information relating to the development and application of chemistry for purposes not prohibited under this Convention."

A more comprehensive nonproliferation measure would be to tie a large portion of international development assistance to nonproliferation goals. (There is a precedent: during the Cold War, US foreign aid policies were keyed closely to blocking Communist influence in the Third World.) One way to do this is to deny aid to countries that do not participate fully in the nonproliferation regimes (e.g., refusing to join and adhere to the NPT, the CWC, or the BWC). Another would be to offer increased aid to induce states to end the regional arms races that stimulate the desire for weapons of mass destruction and to convert military efforts to peaceful development programs.

DISINCENTIVES TO OBTAINING WEAPONS OF MASS DESTRUCTION

ECONOMIC SANCTIONS Related to the sanctions against suppliers (see Appendix Table 5) is a set of sanctions aimed at deterring potential proliferants. Like all disincentives, sanctions are intended to make acquiring weapons of mass destruction seem less than worthwhile. Should a country move toward acquiring the weapons, or violate provisions of agreements not to acquire them, other countries may apply sanctions in an effort to enforce compliance with nonproliferation norms.[4]

---

[4] The IAEA Statute, the CWC, and the BWC all explicitly invite members to bring treaty violations to the attention of the UN Security Council.

Appendix Table 6 summarizes legislative bases for US sanction policies against proliferant nations. In addition, the president can act to mobilize international cooperation on nonproliferation. Through executive branch powers to conduct foreign aid and trade policies, the president can selectively apply what amounts to export controls to specific countries. Through bilateral diplomatic exchanges, he can encourage other nations to restrain their exports. Likewise, he can threaten potential proliferants with economic or other sanctions under his foreign policy powers. For example, US diplomatic initiatives played a major role in the 1970s in persuading South Korea and Taiwan to reverse apparently nascent nuclear weapon programs. The effectiveness of legislated export controls and sanctions depends on conscientious enforcement by the executive branch, and the president can usually waive sanctions at his discretion.

In addition to his diplomatic responsibilities, the president also manages the US intelligence agencies. Intelligence plays a key role in identifying which nations should be subject to special export limitations, in discovering the actual end uses of exported goods, and in monitoring the exports of other nations to potential proliferants. Along with presidential management, congressional oversight can help set US intelligence priorities in these areas.

DIPLOMATIC AND MILITARY RESPONSES Beyond economic sanctions, which could be applied to proliferant nations as well as to suppliers, disincentives might include a variety of threatened responses that would make owning and using weapons of mass destruction seem less attractive. Coercive—or threatened—responses to proliferant states include:

- adversaries equipping themselves with comparable weapons or with effective defenses against them,
- countervailing military alliances,
- diplomatic isolation,
- trade embargoes,
- bilateral or multilateral promises to defend or assist victims of aggression or use of weapons of mass destruction,
- collective international assistance to victims of aggression or use of weapons of mass destruction, and
- military response to acquisition or use of the weapons.

The effectiveness of many of these threatened actions will depend, like other nonproliferation measures, on the degree of international cooperation behind them. The presence of a strong international norm against acquiring or using the weapons will be especially important to achieve cooperation in implementing the more severe measures.

Preparations to carry out such measures may be seen as efforts not only to deter further proliferation, but to manage the consequences of proliferation when it occurs. Military responses are discussed at greater length in the section below on possible responses to proliferation.

LIMITING PROLIFERATION FROM THE FORMER SOVIET UNION   Most of the policy tools described so far in this chapter will be relevant to the republics of the former Soviet Union, but the breakup of the Soviet Union has led to new kinds of proliferation risks. The extent to which the former Soviet republics will disseminate technology, materials, and expertise for producing nuclear, chemical, and biological weapons (as well as ballistic missiles) is still far from certain.

The situation in the former Soviet Union is only partially amenable to outside influences. Nevertheless, the United States and other nations can take steps to encourage favorable outcomes. In 1991–1994, Congress and the administration attempted to help limit these risks by budgeting $400 million each year (beginning with the Nunn-Lugar Soviet Threat Reduction Act of 1991) to assist former Soviet demilitarization.

If weapons of mass destruction remain under effective central Russian control, their export seems unlikely. But the same sorts of civil disorder and governmental breakdown that could lead to the diversion of weapons or key components could also foster the sale of such goods abroad. With or without cooperation from officials in the former Soviet states, US and other foreign intelligence services may be able to help monitor and stop illicit transactions.

The effectiveness of global export controls will be greatly weakened unless Russia and the other former Soviet states join the full set of Western non-proliferation control regimes: the Nuclear Suppliers Group, the Australia Group, and the MTCR. Some progress has been made in this direction with Russia already in the Nuclear Suppliers Group, vowing to become a de facto member of the MTCR, and promising to adhere to the Australia Group guidelines.

A study prepared jointly by the US National Academy of Sciences and the Russian Academy of Sciences has recommended several ways that the two nations may cooperate in controlling exports, including refining the two countries' respective lists of what items require export controls, and deciding jointly which enterprises or "projects of concern" should not receive restricted technologies.[5]

The other newly independent states of the former Soviet Union should also be brought into the nonproliferation regimes. These nations also need to develop effective export control systems. The United States has offered several million dollars in Nunn-Lugar funds for this purpose to each of the four republics retaining Soviet nuclear weapons, and has so far committed about $900 million to specific programs in each of the republics.

At the Moscow summit in January 1994, President Clinton and Russian President Yeltsin signed a joint "Memorandum of Intent" on "Cooperation in the Area of Export Control," saying their governments intended to cooperate in "any or all" of six areas intended to improve nonproliferation export controls and that they may establish expert working groups to carry out their intent. It is too soon to tell whether these actions will be taken or whether they will result in concrete improvements in the Russian control system. Moreover, Russia could move in an uncooperative direction.

The United States and other nations have supported the creation in Moscow and Kiev of International Science and Technology Centers, intended to help establish meaningful, nonmilitary work for scientists and engineers who might otherwise be tempted to accept foreign weapons work to earn a living. Joint projects between US and former Soviet laboratories and firms might be another contribution to that goal. Efficient enforcement of laws and regulations in countries of the former Soviet Union that restrict the sharing of weapons knowledge may help. Overall improvement in the economies of the states that emerged from the former Soviet Union is probably the best hope for discouraging this kind of emigration.

---

[5] US National Academy of Sciences and Russian Academy of Sciences, "Dual Use Technologies and Export Administration in the Post Cold War Era" (Washington, D.C.: National Academy of Sciences, April 1, 1993), p. 20.

Strategies of Monitoring and Response

The ability to respond to programs to develop weapons of mass destruction depends first upon the ability to detect such programs. Detection is accomplished through monitoring programs, which are based on satellites and other remote sensing equipment; tips from knowledgeable individuals; careful review of imports of dual-use equipment; and on-ground inspections of facilities that have the potential to make weapons, or that are suspected of doing so.

Once a program to develop weapons of mass destruction has been detected, potential responses range from economic and trade sanctions to military action. A credible threat made in advance to take action against proliferant nations may also serve as a disincentive to develop weapons of mass destruction.

This section discusses the means of monitoring for programs to develop nuclear, chemical, and biological weapons and delivery systems, and what can be done when such a program is discovered.

MONITORING FOR PROLIFERATION PROGRAMS

The various weapons of mass destruction addressed in this book are based on very different technical principles and require distinct sets of industrial capabilities. Monitoring the proliferation of weapons of mass destruction, or, conversely, monitoring compliance with nonproliferation agreements, depends on detecting and identifying various indicators or "signatures" associated with the development, production, deployment, or use of weapons of mass destruction. Some signatures can be detected with remote instruments. For example, an underground test explosion of a nuclear weapon creates shock waves distinct from those generated by an earthquake, which may be detected by seismic equipment in other countries. Missiles that are test-fired can be seen by satellite. Some signatures of mass destruction weapon programs, however, are evident only through an on-site inspection.

Unilateral intelligence collection efforts can seek to exploit these signatures with the use of remote or covertly placed instruments—for example, satellites that can take high-resolution photographs. Multilateral verification regimes—typically operating within the framework of a negotiated treaty—can make provision for states to voluntarily open their facilities to cooperative on-site inspection in addition to sanctioning the use of remote instrumentation.[6]

Both unilateral and cooperative approaches have their strengths. A cooperative regime might offer direct access to facilities that would be difficult to inspect in any other way, but access may be strictly limited. Moreover, the inspected party knows the type of instrumentation and procedures to be used by inspecting parties, and may be able to defeat the inspections. Intelligence collection efforts conducted outside the framework of a negotiated agreement would probably not have the degree of access to any specific site that would be provided by a cooperative on-site inspection regime, but they might have other advantages such as breadth of coverage. Moreover, they would not be constrained by pre-negotiated procedures, and they might be able to gather information about sites where on-site inspection would be denied. However, if unilateral intelligence efforts involved the covert placement of sensors in the territory of the inspected party, such efforts would probably be viewed as a violation of sovereignty, creating political tensions if detected.

Unilateral and multilateral approaches are not mutually exclusive. Indeed, they will be most effective if used synergistically. For example, unilateral intelligence efforts might trigger a challenge inspection. However, many of the signatures discussed below are likely to be ambiguous, if they are detected at all. Deciding on appropriate responses in the face of incomplete or ambiguous information will pose great challenges for nonproliferation policy, as will mobilizing effective domestic and international support for those responses.

NUCLEAR WEAPONS All facilities for producing weapon-grade nuclear material have unique features amenable to detection by intrusive on-site inspection. Many have distinctive signatures that are detectable remotely, although facilities for some approaches to producing fissile material might not be readily detectable.

The vast majority of fissile material in non-nuclear weapon states is safeguarded by a comprehensive system of material accountancy and control administered by the IAEA. Since members of the NPT (other than the acknowledged nuclear powers) are not permitted to operate

---

[6] In the strategic arms control process between the United States and the Soviet Union, each side agreed not to impede the other's "national technical means of verification," in effect legitimizing the collection of intelligence pertinent to the treaty.

unsafeguarded facilities handling nuclear materials, the existence of any such facilities would probably indicate an illegal weapon program.

IAEA safeguards are not perfect, but they provide high levels of confidence that significant quantities of fissile material have not been diverted from safeguarded nuclear reactors. Diversion would be more difficult to detect from facilities such as fuel fabrication plants, uranium enrichment plants, and plutonium reprocessing facilities. These facilities process large quantities of fissile material in bulk form, as opposed to handling only discrete units such as fuel rods or reactor cores. At present, however, there are no large facilities of this type under comprehensive IAEA safeguards in countries of particular proliferation concern.[7] At least in the short run, the diversion of safeguarded materials poses less of a threat to the nonproliferation regime than the black-market purchase or covert indigenous production of nuclear materials.

As noted in Chapter 3, low- and medium-level gas centrifuge technology for enriching uranium may become increasingly attractive to potential proliferants. Modern, state-of-the-art centrifuges could lead to even smaller, more efficient, and relatively inexpensive facilities that would be more difficult to detect remotely. In the longer run, laser isotope separation techniques and aerodynamic separation may have serious proliferation potential as ways to produce HEU for nuclear weapons. Small laser facilities could enrich uranium to weapon-grade levels in only a few stages. They could therefore prove to be difficult to detect and control if developed in a clandestine program.

Nuclear tests at single kiloton yields or above would probably be detectable by various means, especially if multiple tests were conducted. However, such tests are not necessary to field a workable weapon with reasonably assured yield. Similarly, the deployment of a small number of nuclear weapons might not be easily detected.

CHEMICAL WEAPONS Direct detection of chemical warfare agents in samples taken from a production facility would be a clear indicator of weapon activity, since these agents have almost no civil applications.[8]

---

[7] Brazil has a medium-sized fuel fabrication facility under IAEA safeguards, and South African enrichment facilities are coming under safeguards with South Africa's announced destruction of its nuclear weapons and its accession to the NPT. Neither state is considered an active proliferation threat at present.

[8] Nitrogen mustards have some use in cancer chemotherapy, and phosgene and hydrogen cyanide have industrial applications.

However, considerable access to production facilities is required to collect appropriate samples.

Identifying where to look for evidence of covert production is probably the greatest challenge for monitoring chemical weapon proliferation, since highly reliable technologies to detect chemical agent production from outside a facility are not currently available. Unlike nuclear weapon facilities, which generally exhibit fairly clear signatures, civilian chemical plants have multiple uses, are hundreds of times more numerous than nuclear facilities, and are configured in different ways depending on the process involved. Moreover, many of the chemicals used to make chemical warfare agents are also used to make pharmaceuticals, pesticides, and other commercial products. However, information on plant design and purchase of precursor chemicals may suggest a chemical agent production capability, and may therefore lead to challenge inspections under the CWC.

Indicators at suspect locations that suggest a production capability include visual signatures such as testing munitions and delivery systems; distinctive aspects of plant design and layout, including the use of corrosion-resistant materials and air-purification systems; the presence of chemical agents, precursors, or degradation products in the facility's production line or waste stream; and biochemical evidence of chemical agent exposure (including that due to accidental leaks) in plant workers or in plants and animals near a suspect facility.

BIOLOGICAL WEAPONS Detection of biological and toxin agent production is particularly challenging; clandestine production sites need not be large or distinctive, the equipment involved has legitimate civilian applications, and offensive work can be conducted under the guise of defensive preparations.

Thanks to advances in biotechnology, including improved fermentation equipment and genetic engineering techniques, biological and toxin agents could be made in facilities that are much smaller and less conspicuous than in the past. Moreover, the extreme potency of such agents means that as little as a few kilograms can be militarily significant. Since large amounts of agent can be grown from a freeze-dried seed culture in a period of days to weeks, large stockpiles of agent are not required, although some stocks of the munitions to be filled with these agents would be.

Almost all the equipment involved in biological and toxin weapon development and production is dual-use and hence will not typically indicate weapon activity. Some legitimate biological facilities can convert rapidly to the production of biological warfare agents. In addition, there are no signatures that distinguish clearly between the development of offensive biological agents and work on defensive vaccines, since both activities require the same basic know-how and laboratory techniques at the research and development stage.

However, at present there are relatively few legitimate applications of biological or toxin agents (examples are vaccine production and the clinical use of toxins). With the exception of a few vaccine production plants, such activities are largely confined to sophisticated biomedical facilities not normally found in developing countries, and these facilities generally do not engage in production except on a small scale. Moreover, since the global biotechnology industry is still in its infancy, the number of legitimate activities—from which the illegitimate ones would have to be distinguished—is still relatively small. Sensitive analytical techniques such as polymerase chain reaction analysis or use of monoclonal antibodies can identify trace quantities of biological agents and might be able to do so even after the termination of illicit activities.

However, the existence of such sensitive laboratory techniques does not ensure that an effective on-site inspection regime can be established to detect the production of biological or toxin weapons. (The BWC does not currently provide for monitoring of potential biological weapon programs.) Other factors that must be assessed in establishing such a regime include the likelihood of detecting clandestine production sites, the ability to distinguish prohibited offensive activities from permitted defensive efforts, and the risk of divulging sensitive national-security or proprietary information.

Identifying where to look for evidence of biological agent production is even harder than for chemical agents. Because of the difficulty of detecting clandestine development and production of biological and toxin weapons, effective tracking of such programs will require integrating data from many sources, with a particular emphasis on human intelligence (agents, defectors, and whistle-blowers). Some weaponization signatures (storage of bulk agents, preparation of aerosol dispensers, field testing, etc.) would probably be easier to detect than production signatures, but many such signatures could be concealed or masked by legitimate activities such as biopesticide research and development or use. Production and storage of components for biological weapon munitions might also be masked by activities associated with conventional weapons, such as production of high explosives, bomb casings, or artillery shells. Since excessive secrecy might itself indicate an offensive intent, greater transparency would tend to build confidence in a country's lack of offensive intentions.

DELIVERY SYSTEMS Although individual missiles can be very difficult to detect, a program to develop ballistic missiles is much more visible. The development of intermediate- and long-range ballistic missiles requires extensive flight testing. Test firing and launching of ballistic missiles can be readily seen by satellite.

Some states pursuing a civilian space-launch program may also be developing military missile technology. Even a purely civilian space-launch program provides technology and know-how useful for ballistic missiles. The most important aspects of a missile capability for weapons of mass destruction—range and payload—can usually be inferred from a civil program. (A civil space-launch booster does not need high accuracy; nor does a missile carrying weapons of mass destruction for use against populations.)

On the other hand, certain attributes desired for military applications, such as reliable reentry vehicles, mobility, and ease of operation in the field, require distinct technical approaches for military and civil applications. Although solid-fueled boosters are in some ways more difficult to develop and build than liquid-fueled boosters, they are easier to use in mobile and time-urgent applications. Liquid-fueled boosters were the first used in military applications and are still more common. For example, the Scud missile and its modifications, such as those launched by Iraq in 1991 against targets in Israel and Saudi Arabia, are liquid-fueled.

Combat aircraft are widely accepted as integral to the military forces of developing countries; thus there is no reason to hide their existence. (Individual planes, however, can be hidden.) Modifications made to aircraft to carry weapons of mass destruction, or training given to pilots for their delivery, might, however, be difficult to detect without intrusive inspections.

Of the three delivery systems, cruise missile development and testing will be the hardest to detect. Several types of unmanned aerial vehicles are being developed and marketed for civil purposes, and without inspection rights it will be difficult to discern whether such vehicles have been converted to military purposes.

POSSIBLE RESPONSES

SANCTIONS Mechanisms exist in US law—but are not laid out in international law—to punish states found to have used weapons of mass destruction or to have engaged in activities related to their development. Within the United States, current laws and regulations to deter or punish proliferants stress economic sanctions. However, other measures could be taken, many of which serve not only to deter further proliferation but to help address the consequences of proliferation if it occurs. These measures include:

- embarrassment by exposing illicit activities;
- provision of technical or military assistance to states threatened by weapons of mass destruction;
- development and deployment of active defenses (e.g., missile or air defenses) or passive measures (e.g., gas masks and protective clothing) to protect against the weapons;
- diplomatic isolation of proliferants or formation of countervailing military alliances; and
- withdrawal of US security guarantees.

Like other nonproliferation measures, the effectiveness of these measures will depend on the degree of international cooperation behind them. The presence of strong international norms against acquisition and use of these weapons will be important to getting that cooperation.

At the international level, enforcement of international nonproliferation commitments falls to the United Nations Security Council, which has the authority to respond to "threats to international peace and security" by imposing measures such as sanctions, severance of travel and communication links, diplomatic isolation, or even military action under Chapter VII of the United Nations charter.[9] Actions of the Security Council are binding upon all UN members. Security Council

---

[9] By themselves, international organizations involved with nonproliferation, such as the IAEA, typically can take no punitive action stronger than expelling members found to have violated their commitments to the organization. However, the IAEA can refer evidence of violations to the United Nations Security Council for further action.

enforcement of existing nonproliferation commitments such as the NPT and the 1925 Geneva Protocol could deter further proliferation and strengthen global nonproliferation norms.[10] Conversely, inaction will weaken the nonproliferation regime.

Any UN efforts to enforce treaty commitments will not directly affect those states that have not acceded to these commitments in the first place. However, in January 1992, the Security Council declared the proliferation of weapons of mass destruction to be a threat to international peace and security, opening up at least the possibility of taking action even against proliferants who are not party to global nonproliferation regimes.

MILITARY ACTION One military response to proliferation is to attempt to destroy the means of production of the weapons before they can be fabricated and deployed. A second is to attempt to destroy weapons already built before they can be used. A third is to employ defensive measures to try to neutralize the weapons (either passive measures, such as gas masks and protective suits, or active defenses, such as anti-ballistic missiles). A fourth approach, embodied in Security Council Resolution 687 and related resolutions, is to use or threaten military force to coerce the proliferant into surrendering the weapons and their means of production. Finally, one might force a change of governmental regime to one that would voluntarily forswear the weapons of concern.

Perhaps the first clear example of a military response to a proliferation threat was the Israeli bombing of the Iraqi Osirak nuclear reactor in 1981. This step set back the Iraqi nuclear weapon program but did not end it. The bombing did cause Iraq to do a better job of concealing it. In 1991, as part of Operation Desert Storm, the UN-backed coalition against Iraq attacked and destroyed facilities believed to be connected to Iraqi mass-destruction weapon programs. The UN Security Council required the elimination of all such facilities as part of the cease-fire it imposed on Iraq.

Other types of forcible interference besides direct military attack might include:

- sabotage of equipment or materials before transfer, either on the territory of its supplier or in transit;
- military interdiction of equipment or material; or

---

[10] The UN has never taken action against signatories to the 1925 Geneva Protocol that have violated their agreement not to use chemical or biological weapons.

• sabotage of equipment or materials after import.

The UN Security Council declared in January 1992 that the proliferation of weapons of mass destruction "constitutes a threat to international peace and security." This phrasing, referring to a key clause in the United Nations Charter, makes it conceivable that sometime the Council might approve the use of military force to destroy facilities for producing or storing weapons of mass destruction. Even so, such authority is likely to be highly circumscribed, lest states interpret it as license to attack others with impunity. Moreover, the necessary steps of deliberation, approval, and preparation would give considerable advance notice to the targeted state. An internationally sanctioned strike would therefore be poorly suited for missions requiring surprise.

As a result, states believing their vital interests to be at stake may decide to take unilateral military action against some cases of proliferation. However, if such actions are not sanctioned by the international community—at least after the fact—they may damage the international consensus on cooperative nonproliferation efforts. Nations committing the action may find themselves accused of violating international law. Moreover, an attack may even build sympathy for the victim, ultimately lessening the obstacles to its weapon program. Whether such an attack were internationally sanctioned or not, it would also risk retaliation or even full-scale war by the target country against either the attacking nations or their allies.

WHEN NONPROLIFERATION FAILS
Some analysts argue that further proliferation of weapons of mass destruction is inevitable and that nonproliferation policy is, if anything, counterproductive. Others say that although nonproliferation policies should continue, it is prudent to plan for at least some further proliferation, and to be prepared to try to mitigate its consequences for national and international security. Modifying US force plans and structures to cope with the possible further proliferation of weapons of mass destruction is unquestionably an important task for US policymakers. Recognizing this fact, the Department of Defense has created a counterproliferation policy initiative led by the Office of International Security Policy.

COUNTER-THREATS Deterrent counter-threats may dissuade the proliferant country from using its weapons. Analysts have hypothesized that

Iraq did not use its chemical weapons against coalition troops in the 1991 Gulf War because it feared a US retaliation in kind, a US response with nuclear weapons, or an escalation of the conventional attack to the point of eliminating the Hussein regime; others suggest that Iraq just calculated that there was no useful application available for chemical weapons. Some argue that the possibility of Israeli nuclear retaliation deterred Iraq from using Scud missiles with chemical warheads against Israel.

A POLICY OF ACCEPTANCE FOR NUCLEAR WEAPONS   The current nuclear states could implicitly or explicitly acquiesce in the deployment of nuclear weapons by India, Pakistan, or Israel. They could then offer the newcomers to the nuclear club help in developing stabilizing doctrines of deployment and deterrence. The help might be technical assistance to reduce the vulnerability of their nuclear forces to a disarming first strike from others. Or, it might take the form of technology for tightening centralized control over the weapons themselves and for preventing unauthorized use, theft, or accidents.

Promoting safer deployment of weapons of mass destruction would be inconsistent with a stated goal of a global ban on possession—as in the cases of chemical and biological weapons. But in the case of nuclear weapons, the policy might "grandfather" nuclear arms deemed to be irreversibly deployed, as the NPT does those of the United States, Russia, Britain, France, and China.

A policy of acceptance might mitigate post-proliferation risks, but it would also tend to encourage further proliferation by showing that successful evasion of the obstacles to proliferation can eventually lead to legitimacy as a member of the nuclear club. It also would strongly discourage present nuclear weapon states from reducing their arsenals. Technical assistance on safety and security measures could also lead the new nuclear power to integrate its weapons more tightly into its military forces, keep them at higher levels of alert, and think of them as more usable instruments of force.

Chapter 6

Nonproliferation Trends and Efforts

Prerequisites to Effective Nonproliferation Policy

If nonproliferation policy is to succeed, it must receive substantial international cooperation. Cooperation is necessary because no single nation or small group of nations can prevent proliferation or contain its consequences. Cooperation is possible because many countries have come to recognize that the proliferation of nuclear, chemical, and biological weapons poses a genuine threat to all nations. However, since states will not always agree on nonproliferation measures, maintaining and acting on an effective consensus will require each participating country to give up some freedom to act independently.

Some analysts argue that containing proliferation in the long run will require a far deeper level of international cooperation than has been achieved to date, one that builds international institutions for a much more cooperative global security regime. Others argue that the international political system is inevitably anarchic and the degree of cooperation needed to contain proliferation cannot be achieved.

In any case, the end of the Cold War has opened up new opportunities for cooperative nonproliferation policies. One promising sign is the revitalization of the United Nations Security Council. Progress has also been made with the signing of the Chemical Weapons Convention and the strengthening of various multilateral groups that have formed for the purpose of controlling the spread of proliferation-sensitive technology: the Nuclear Suppliers Group, to control exports of nuclear technology; and the Australia Group, to control materials useful for chemical and biological weapons; and the MTCR, to restrict traffic in missile systems and missile technology. (These agreements are discussed in Chapter 5.)

If US nonproliferation policy is to succeed, the United States must give it high priority. With its leadership role in the world community, the United States has the opportunity and the ability to mobilize international nonproliferation efforts. Free of previously overriding Cold War security concerns, the United States can now attach greater priority to nonproliferation. Doing so, however, is not without costs. Nonproliferation may conflict with economic goals, as export promotion is balanced against export controls. Promoting openness, transparency, and verification of nonproliferation commitments, on the one hand, conflicts with maintaining the secrecy of national-security or proprietary information, on the other. Nonproliferation efforts may also conflict with other foreign policy objectives. For example, would the United States consider changing its relationship with Israel to pressure that state to give up a nuclear arsenal it believes is essential to its security? Or, how prominently should nonproliferation figure in US relations with China, a regional power whose cooperation the United States seeks in other diplomatic and economic arenas?

As noted in Chapter 5, strategies for inhibiting proliferation build on four broad elements: practical obstacles, punitive measures, rewards, and global or regional security improvements to reduce the perceived needs for the weapons. The increasing international flow of technical knowledge, high-technology goods, and trained specialists is eroding the ability of the United States and its allies to put technical hurdles in the path of countries bent on acquiring weapons of mass destruction. This puts greater weight on the diplomatic, political, organizational, and economic costs and benefits that bear on a state's decision to pursue such weapons. Reducing the incentives and raising the costs are both important in persuading states that it is in their own interest not to pursue weapons of mass destruction. External obstacles and disincentives can also help by buying time for diplomatic or political measures to forestall proliferation.

Against this backdrop, the following sections review recent trends favoring nonproliferation, and trends fostering proliferation. The last part of the chapter then looks at current priorities in US and international nonproliferation efforts.

Trends Favoring Nonproliferation

RISING NORMS AGAINST PROLIFERATION

An international consensus seems to be growing that the further spread of nuclear weapons should be stopped, and that chemical and biological weapons should be eliminated completely. Many governments have declared renewed commitments to nonproliferation. Strengthened norms could help both to deter potential proliferants and to strengthen international cooperation in nonproliferation efforts.

The past few years have brought a big increase in the number of parties to the nuclear Nonproliferation Treaty, which rose from 138 at the end of 1989 to 167 by January 1, 1995. Two of the nuclear weapon states that did not originally join the NPT, China and France, have joined in the last few years, as has South Africa, formerly a hold-out that produced nuclear weapons outside the NPT. Although three NPT non-signatories—Israel, India, and Pakistan—are believed to have actual or potential nuclear weapon capabilities, no new states have declared that they have nuclear weapons since 1964, when China did; and no non-nuclear members of the NPT have "gone nuclear," although a few have moved in that direction (see Chapter 2).

Given their reductions in strategic intercontinental nuclear forces and withdrawal of shorter-range tactical nuclear weapons the United States and Russia can now say that they are meeting their NPT obligation to "pursue negotiations in good faith on effective measures relating to cessation of the nuclear arms race." At the 1995 NPT review and extension conference, however, many NPT parties will argue that the nuclear weapon states have not done enough to warrant an indefinite treaty extension.

END OF THE COLD WAR

The end of the Cold War has strengthened support for nonproliferation. Besides fostering a new level of cooperation between the United States and Russia, the end of the East-West conflict has made possible changes in national priorities and policy emphases. Nonproliferation policies may still conflict with other policy goals, but they need no longer be subordinated to Cold War objectives. In addition, foreign policy and intelligence resources are being redirected from Cold War efforts to deal with proliferation.

Should Russia revert to a foreign policy that is seriously threatening to Western interests, nonproliferation would be set back since future efforts will require significant cooperation between the United States and Russia, not just parallel policies in certain areas.

RECENT REVERSALS OF NATIONAL POLICIES

Recent rollbacks in the nuclear weapon programs of Argentina, Brazil, South Africa, and (albeit involuntarily) Iraq follow decisions in earlier decades by Sweden, South Korea, and Taiwan to halt programs that might have led to acquisition. Such reversals, however, are themselves reversible, as exemplified by North Korea's threat to withdraw from the NPT (see Chapter 2).

GROWING COOPERATION IN EXPORT CONTROLS

Several multilateral groups have formed to control the export of equipment or materials that might be used in the production of weapons of mass destruction or of missiles. These control regimes have been strengthened in the past few years by covering additional items and by expanding their membership. Particularly notable is the April 1992 decision of the 28-member Nuclear Suppliers Group to require importers of nuclear technology to accept monitoring by the IAEA of their entire nuclear programs, not just of the particular facilities built with imported technology.

This action leaves China as the only supplier of nuclear technology that does not require "full-scope safeguards" as a condition of sale. By requiring full-scope safeguards, exporters prevent states from acquiring expertise in safeguarded facilities and using it to build and operate other facilities that are not open to international inspection or controls.

UN ACTIONS IN IRAQ

The UN Security Council resolutions that required the dismantling of Iraq's programs for weapons of mass destruction alluded positively to international nonproliferation and disarmament treaties, setting useful precedents in demonstrating international resolve against proliferation. The Security Council also took on long-term on-site monitoring in Iraq to ensure that it does not resume producing such weapons.

CHEMICAL WEAPONS CONVENTION

The two largest chemical weapon powers, the United States and Russia, have made a commitment to destroy their chemical weapon arsenals and related development and production facilities. The Iraqi chemical arsenal has been completely dismantled under UN supervision, and the UN has established long-term monitoring of Iraq's chemical industry.

The Chemical Weapons Convention, signed by more than 140 states in early 1993, bans the development, production, and possession of chemical weapons, as well as their use. Despite some lingering doubts about verification, the convention strengthens the international consensus that chemical weapons are illegitimate. Thus, if some nation were to use chemical weapons in the future, the international community would be likely to react more strongly than it did at the time of Iraq's use against Iran in the 1980s.

BIOLOGICAL WEAPONS CONVENTION

In the wake of the Russian admission in 1992 that the Soviet Union had violated the Biological Weapons Convention, the United States, the United Kingdom, and Russia have agreed on a program to inspect each other's biological facilities. States that have joined the convention disagree over the feasibility and desirability of a formal verification regime, but are meeting in 1995 to consider potential verification measures.

Trends Favoring Proliferation

The end of the Cold War has the potential not only to strengthen nonproliferation efforts, but also to weaken restraints against proliferation. This is most apparent in the republics of the former Soviet Union. In addition, countries that formerly had Soviet or US security guarantees may now feel more vulnerable, increasing their motivation to acquire weapons of mass destruction.

PERSISTENCE OF REGIONAL CONFLICTS

Long-standing regional conflicts in South Asia, East Asia, and the Middle East have created high-risk zones for proliferation. In South Asia, India and Pakistan have failed to resolve their ethnic and territorial dispute over Kashmir, and India feels threatened by China, its nuclear neighbor to the northeast. In East Asia, relations between Taiwan and Beijing are a source of tension, as are developments on the Korean peninsula.

In the Middle East, the peace process does not promise an early end to the Arab-Israeli conflict, and even independent of Israel, the Islamic countries would probably continue to arm against one another. [1]

Proliferation of conventional arms, fueled by these regional conflicts and by the glut of military industrial capacity and weapon stockpiles left in the wake of the Cold War, can stimulate a quest for weapons of mass destruction as "equalizers." At the same time, international transfers of advanced combat aircraft and the spread of missile technology are strengthening military capabilities for delivering weapons of mass destruction.

SPREADING TECHNOLOGY AND INDUSTRIALIZATION

Economic and technological development increases national wealth and enhances industrial capabilities useful for indigenous production of weapons of mass destruction and their delivery systems. Development also increases the number of potential foreign suppliers of skill and technology to proliferant nations. Consequently, the industrially advanced countries will find it increasingly difficult to control weapon proliferation by limiting exports of key technologies or materials.

In fact, the dissemination of technologies that can help produce weapons of mass destruction may need to be not merely tolerated but encouraged if developing populations are to improve their health, environment, and standards of living. This applies particularly to chemical and biological technologies. "Dual-use" technologies that can contribute both to military and civil products can often be used in a host of applications, such as computing, metal-forming, and diagnostic testing. Thus, in some cases (where the technologies are already widely disseminated) controls on dual-use technologies will prove infeasible, while in other cases (where vital non-weapon-related activities would be constrained) they may be undesirable.

These difficulties notwithstanding, export controls remain an important nonproliferation tool. For example, although Iraq's indigenous industrial base was more capable than most outsiders realized, Iraq still had to import much of the equipment used in its weapon facilities.

---

[1] Arab and Iranian disputes with Turkey, a NATO member, have the potential to involve the United States directly.

This level of import was made feasible by Iraqi oil revenues combined with the willingness of foreign manufacturers to supply equipment and the lack of effective export controls in the supplying countries.

RESISTANCE TO DISCRIMINATORY REGIMES
A few developing countries, notably India and Iran, object to attempts to deny them nuclear and missile-related technologies that are accepted as legitimate for other countries. Most nations, however, are willing to live with the two-tiered, nuclear/non-nuclear structure of the nuclear NPT. This issue does not arise for the Chemical and Biological Weapons Conventions, both of which apply equally to all treaty parties.

WEAKENED TABOO AGAINST CHEMICAL WEAPONS
The 1925 Geneva Protocol prohibits the use of chemical and biological agents in warfare. This ban was observed in most of the conflicts following its entry into force, including World War II (except when Japan, then a non-party, used chemical and biological weapons in China, as described in Chapter 2). More recent instances of chemical weapon use have weakened the international norm against such use. In particular, Iraqi use of chemical weapons against Iran in the 1980s may have led some defense planners to believe that chemical weapons can be a useful military tool.

RISKS FROM THE BREAKUP OF THE SOVIET UNION
The breakup of the Soviet Union and the shakiness of government authority in the former Soviet republics could exacerbate many proliferation problems. As noted in Chapters 1 and 4, Belarus, Kazakhstan, and Ukraine have begun to transfer all nuclear warheads on their territories to Russia (in accord with the May 1992 Lisbon Protocol to the START agreement), and they have all acceded to the NPT as non-nuclear weapon states. But many missiles and warheads remain in place, and actual removal will take several years. Should the republics choose in the meantime to become nuclear powers (in violation of their START and NPT commitments), they could seize the weapons and adapt them to that purpose. Alternatively, they might dismantle the weapons and then fail to control the fissile material properly.

All Soviet "tactical" (non-intercontinental) nuclear weapons have been pulled into Russia. The question of whether Russia will develop a pronounced authoritarian trend or will fragment is still unsettled, as is the question of whether the custodial system for the thousands of former Soviet nuclear weapons and hundreds of tons of nuclear weapon materials (HEU and separated plutonium) will break down.

Despite some rumors, there is as yet no serious evidence that Soviet nuclear weapons have been sold to other countries, nor that chemical or biological weapons have been exported.

There is also no clear evidence that former Soviet technical personnel with knowledge of how to build weapons of mass destruction have emigrated to other countries, though there have been reports of some attempts at recruitment. Such scientists or technicians might not be essential to a developing country's weapon program, but they might provide useful guidance about what works and what does not, thus speeding the development of weapons.

The most immediate risk in the former Soviet Union may be the export of information, equipment, or materials. The major areas of concern are dual-use technologies and materials, and fissile materials. Russia and the other former Soviet republics face severe shortages of hard currency: they are trying to establish market systems of production and trade, but the legal infrastructure to regulate such activities is not yet fully developed. It is possible that some exporting enterprises may be unaware of the proliferation risks of particular goods; others may intentionally take advantage of poorly enforced or corruptly administered export control laws. A Ukrainian firm reportedly has already exported tens of tons of hafnium and zirconium, metals which are on the Nuclear Suppliers Group list of restricted dual-use items.

Governments can differ about which exports constitute a proliferation risk. In 1993, Russia and the United States faced off over a Russian plan to sell India cryogenic rocket engine technology. After the United States imposed trade sanctions, Russia agreed to limit the technology transfer and to adhere to the US interpretation of MTCR guidelines. In 1994 and 1995, there were further disputes over Russian sales of nuclear material and technology to Iran.

Fissile materials might in one way or another be diverted from former Soviet weapon stockpiles or from production facilities. The possibility of a breakdown in the Russian custodial system for weapons is mentioned above. A breakdown in the control of material production facilities, leading to theft and export of fissile materials, is also conceivable. Outside Russia, some important former Soviet production facilities remain; of particular concern is a fast breeder reactor, capable of producing over 100 kg (220 lbs.) of weapon-grade plutonium per year, at Aktau, Kazakhstan.

There have been several seizures of nuclear material suspected to have come from the former Soviet Union. In 1994, German officials made four seizures of smuggled weapon-grade material. The largest seizure was a half pound of plutonium smuggled on a plane from Moscow that was to be the first part of a total sale of nine pounds of plutonium for $250 million. The other three seizures were of much smaller quantities; presumably they were samples to show the seller's capability to obtain weapon-grade material. In late 1994, Czech authorities arrested nuclear smugglers with about six pounds of highly enriched plutonium. Two of the smugglers were from Belarus and Ukraine, but the source of the material was not known.

A longer-term possibility is that some former Soviet republics might utilize their own expertise, equipment, or materials to develop indigenous weapon programs. Unlike other new proliferants, such countries might inherit, rather than have to import, some critical weapon technologies. Given the current economic conditions throughout the former Soviet Union, new nuclear weapon programs do not seem to be an immediate threat. Chemical or biological weapons would be easier to develop. Kazakhstan has inherited chemical and biological weapon facilities from the former Soviet military complex; Uzbekistan has inherited test ranges for both types of weapons.

Current US and International Efforts to Stem Proliferation

NUCLEAR NONPROLIFERATION TREATY EXTENSION
Recent nonproliferation efforts centered on the UN April 1995 conference to review and extend the NPT. The treaty stipulates that 25 years following entry into force, its parties must meet to extend the treaty indefinitely, for a fixed period, or for fixed periods. Before the conference, many non-nuclear weapon states criticized the nuclear weapon states for not meeting their treaty obligations under Articles IV and VI. Article IV promotes the development of nuclear energy and compels treaty parties with advanced nuclear technology to "cooperate in contributing...to the further development of the applications of nuclear energy for peaceful purposes, especially in the territories of non-nuclear-weapon states." Some developing nations, such as Iran, argue that the nuclear powers have refused to provide technical assistance

for budding nuclear programs even though the recipient states are in good standing with the NPT and the IAEA.

In Article VI, the NPT parties undertook to negotiate measures in good faith to end the nuclear arms race and to work toward nuclear disarmament as well as general and complete disarmament. US officials have promoted the US record of recent arms control initiatives, particularly the completion of the START accords and a moratorium on nuclear testing. But critics say the United States and the other nuclear weapon states have not achieved enough progress towards nuclear disarmament. They call for more far-reaching measures, including a comprehensive nuclear test ban treaty, a treaty banning the production of fissile materials for nuclear weapons, and pledges by the nuclear weapon states never to use nuclear weapons first and never to use or threaten to use nuclear weapons against non-nuclear weapon states. (Such pledges are called "negative security assurances.")

All the nuclear weapon states advocate extending the treaty indefinitely, arguing that a nonproliferation norm would be more difficult to establish and sustain if the treaty were scheduled to end at some future date. If the treaty were only temporary, they say, nations would be less likely to join, and in tense regions nations might try to gain or retain a nuclear weapon capability in the near term if they knew that their neighbors could legally obtain nuclear weapons as soon as the treaty extension expired.

Many non-nuclear weapon states fear that extending the NPT indefinitely will remove the incentive for the nuclear weapon states to meet their Article IV and VI obligations, thereby making the treaty permanently discriminatory. If the treaty were extended for a series of fixed periods, such as 25-year periods, they argue, the nuclear weapon states would need to continue progress toward nuclear disarmament in order to retain the support of the non-nuclear weapon states and keep the treaty in force when it came up for the extension.

COMPREHENSIVE NUCLEAR TEST BAN

Efforts to limit or ban test explosions of nuclear weapons, discussed for decades, have led to the 1963 Limited Test Ban Treaty, which permits tests at underground sites, and the 1974 Threshold Test Ban Treaty and the 1976 Peaceful Nuclear Explosions Treaty, which capped the yields of US and Soviet (now Russian) tests at less than 150 kilotons. These treaties all call for continuing negotiations to ban all nuclear weapon tests, but such talks bore little fruit until 1994 when the UN's Conference on Disarmament agreed to negotiations on a Comprehensive Test Ban Treaty and produced a draft treaty.

The treaty could be completed in 1995, but several issues remain to be resolved. China may want to retain the right to conduct peaceful nuclear explosions, a position opposed by many nations who worry that it is difficult to distinguish between nuclear weapon tests and tests of nuclear explosives designed for non-military uses. The United States and Russia have explored the possibility of retaining the right to conduct "hydronuclear explosions" or very low-yield tests. Britain and France want to be permitted to conduct tests to confirm the "safety and reliability" of their stockpiles. The majority of negotiating parties want all nuclear explosions banned, regardless of their size, nature, or purpose, and some nations want to prohibit treaty parties from even preparing nuclear tests to help deter potential violators.

Momentum for a comprehensive test ban grew in 1993 and 1994 as the NPT extension conference neared, but there was not time to complete the treaty before the NPT renewal conference.

ENHANCING EXPORT CONTROLS

Intelligence collection and analysis are important in identifying and tracking proliferation activities. The US intelligence community has established an office for this purpose. To be most effective, however, intelligence analysts must make full use of information available from other US government agencies and from open sources. In addition, officials and experts outside the intelligence community play a role in producing export control lists of goods and target countries. The fullest possible cooperation among these players is essential for the government as a whole to develop the most effective policies. No technical fixes can substitute for such cooperation. Several options are available for facilitating communication among policy-makers and improving the base of information and analysis on which they draw.

One option is to create a common database through which all the involved analysts share the widest possible range of information available. For example, data from export license approvals and denials, financial transactions, customs discoveries and investigations, insurance underwriting, the trade press, and intelligence sources might be combined to reveal the kinds of clandestine procurement networks Iraq used to supply its nuclear weapon program.

Another option is to upgrade the information system supporting the export control license evaluation process currently conducted by the US Department of Commerce and other agencies. An upgraded system could provide evaluators with all information potentially relevant to the license application. For example, it could allow reviewing analysts of any agency to which licenses are referred to extract from a computer database information about previous relevant decisions or other current applications involving similar commodities, sellers, buyers, or proposed end-users and end-uses.

A third option is to require the Commerce Department to publish information about each license issued to export any nuclear dual-use item. Advocates of transparency in licensing decisions have been interested primarily in public accountability: "Pushing export licensing into the light of day would encourage the exporters to be honest, encourage the government to be careful, and allow the public to find out whether US exports are undermining national security."[2]

The US Office of Technology Assessment also proposed strengthening the coordination of export license evaluations among the Departments of Commerce and Defense, and other agencies; increasing the awareness of exporters about the export control program, and encouraging them to report approaches by buyers who may be trying to evade the regulations; and improving enforcement of export controls, including pre-license checks and post-shipment verifications on the end-users named in export license applications.[3]

In March 1992, the Nuclear Suppliers Group agreed to adopt common export controls on a list of nuclear-related dual-use materials, equipment, and technologies. The Department of Energy's Office of Arms Control is computerizing information sharing for the NSG agreement. Thus far, at least 20 members of the group have agreed to install test terminals for this system. Such a network would offer a variety of opportunities for increased coordination among the suppliers. For example, license denial information could be especially useful to governments without the extensive export control infrastructure and intelligence resources of some of the larger members of the Nuclear Suppliers

---

[2] Gary Milhollin, "Licensing Mass Destruction: US Exports to Iraq, 1985–1990," manuscript, Wisconsin Project on Nuclear Arms Control, June 1991, p. 14.
[3] US Congress, Office of Technology Assessment, *Export Controls and Nonproliferation Policy*, OTA-ISS-596 (Washington, D.C.: US Government Printing Office, May 1994).

Group. The network could also serve as a funnel for contributions of national intelligence services to the multilateral group.

The reference information in the proposed Nuclear Suppliers Group database would also include the export guidelines of the Missile Technology Control Regime and the control list of the Australia Group (both the Australia Group and the MTCR are described in Chapter 5). Other than furnishing up-to-date details about those regimes, the proposed database would play no further role in coordinating the suppliers.

Nevertheless, the basic mechanisms of the proposed suppliers' database could be extended to the Australia Group and the MTCR. This step would be most useful in combination with agreements in those regimes to report export denials, as the suppliers' do. If the political difficulties could be overcome, a single proliferation export-control database seems technically feasible, since there is a high degree of overlapping membership among these groups (Figure 6 in Chapter 5).

Whether by means of a networked database or through other means of communication, sharing intelligence data about unscrupulous suppliers, buying and financing operations, questionable agents, and suspicious end-users is an important means by which supplier groups can coordinate their export controls. The immediate goal of increased intelligence and other information sharing among governments would be to enhance their export controls. At the same time, greater public information about proliferation activities could help mobilize international support for the whole range of nonproliferation policies: not only coercive actions against violators of nonproliferation norms, but internal and external pressures on governments to renounce weapons of mass destruction and adhere to the nonproliferation regimes.

Newly industrializing countries that are not members of the established export control groups are also becoming possible suppliers to proliferants. Including such nations in multilateral export control arrangements would make the new suppliers less likely to contribute to proliferation. At the same time, their participation in international controls would help counter the claim that such controls are discriminatory measures intended to preserve the economic and military advantages of the more prosperous nations.

VERIFIED CESSATION OF PRODUCTION OF NUCLEAR WEAPON FISSILE MATERIALS

In 1994 diplomats at the UN Conference on Disarmament in Geneva agreed to negotiate a ban on the production of fissile materials for nuclear weapons, but failed to agree on a specific negotiating mandate. While all delegations agreed that the mandate should include fissile material production, some delegations from the Non-Aligned Movement wanted the talks to cover existing stockpiles of fissile materials, not just future production. The idea was ultimately to create a regime to draw down nuclear stockpiles. Some nuclear weapon states adamantly oppose broadening the mandate, and the impasse has not yet been resolved.

Another unresolved issue concerns the production of weapon-usable fissile materials for peaceful purposes. Japan has begun to build a large nuclear energy complex based on plutonium fuel, which can also be used to make nuclear weapons. This plan has been widely criticized by nonproliferation advocates.

NEGATIVE SECURITY ASSURANCES

Negative security assurances—pledges not to use or threaten to use nuclear weapons—have been on the agenda of the Conference on Disarmament for 15 years, but little progress has been made. The five declared nuclear weapon states have all made unilateral assurances over the years, but have refused to join a formal international agreement. Britain, France, and the United States consider the unilateral assurances to be sufficient and want to limit the assurances to NPT parties or nations abiding by other legally-binding international agreements. Russia supports a multilateral agreement, but also supports a five-party agreement among the declared nuclear weapon states. China wants to include negative security assurances in a larger nuclear agreement that includes a general pledge of no first use of nuclear weapons and other measures.

SECURITY IMPROVEMENTS AND POSITIVE SECURITY GUARANTEES

Coercive measures alone are unlikely to be sufficient to stop states from acquiring weapons of mass destruction. In the long term, the best hope for nonproliferation lies in a consensus among potential proliferants that they should jointly refrain from acquiring these weapons.

Improvements in security that reduce the perceived need for or appeal of the weapons can help prevent or limit proliferation. Measures to improve security might include:

- regional agreements in which potential military adversaries mutually renounce weapons of mass destruction;
- transparency and confidence-building measures to help verify that potential adversaries are forgoing such weapons;
- broader regional or global arms control arrangements that reduce threats of conventional war;
- a commitment by the members (or permanent members) of the UN Security Council to help defend any UN member state that is subjected to conventional military attack;
- regional security arrangements that reduce the risk of war; and
- global security arrangements that reduce the chances of attack from outside the region.

ADDRESSING MOTIVATIONS
Persuading potential proliferants of the benefits of going without weapons of mass destruction has been partially successful in the past. More than 165 non-nuclear countries have ratified or acceded to the NPT, many of which are technically capable of building nuclear weapons; most that are capable are refraining. The Chemical Weapons Convention has been signed by numerous nations that could, but almost certainly will not, acquire chemical weapons.

Still, some countries have refused to rule out the nuclear option, and others (Iraq and possibly North Korea) have violated their agreement to abstain. Several declined initially to join the Chemical Convention, although they may yet be brought in. Some are suspected of violating their obligations under the Biological Convention.

In its 1977 report, *Nuclear Proliferation and Safeguards*, the US Office of Technology Assessment found that

> the technical and economic barriers to proliferation are declining as accessibility to nuclear weapon material becomes more widespread. Consequently, the decision whether or not to acquire a nuclear weapon capability has become increasingly a political one. The choice will turn on whether a nation views the possession of such a capability as being, on balance, in its national interest.

The conclusion that, in the long run, motivations are key still holds true. Motivations are especially important for chemical and biological weapons because the technologies for making them are relatively widely accessible.

Factors that make it difficult to persuade some nations to forgo weapons of mass destruction include not only the perceived military value of the weapons (see Chapter 1), but also the double standards which discriminate against all but the most powerful nations; domino effects; and regional rivalries.

Aspiring ballistic missile owners feel that they are being asked to accept an international double standard: the advanced powers now deploying ballistic missiles have the right to do so, but newcomers to the club are not welcome. Moreover, curbs on longer-range ballistic missiles are complicated by the fact that their design is close to that of space-launch vehicles. India, which has both space-launch and ballistic missile programs, resents US attempts to block foreign exports to its space program that might also be useful to its missile program.

India has also complained vigorously that it is hypocritical of the United States and the other nuclear powers to deny the rights of non-nuclear nations to acquire the weapons without giving up their own. Although Argentina and Brazil are moving toward participation in the Treaty of Tlatelolco (making Latin America a nuclear-free zone) and have accepted IAEA safeguards on all their nuclear facilities, but Brazil has refused to join the NPT on the grounds that it is discriminatory.

In the case of Iraq, the international community has reached an unusual consensus that Iraq is unfit to own nuclear weapons. But neither Iraq nor India nor most other nations accept what they see as the implication that all but the five acknowledged nuclear powers are unqualified to handle the responsibilities of nuclear guardianship.

A second perception of double standards stems from the variability of past US nonproliferation policies. From the US point of view, failing to make serious efforts to block Israeli acquisition of nuclear weapons or to enforce sanctions against Pakistan in the 1980s in response to its nuclear program reflect the dilemmas of conflicting policy objectives. From the point of view of some other countries, however, it reflects a willingness to look the other way when the proliferant is a friend of the United States—to select what proliferation is acceptable.

The history of double standards, real or perceived, will in some cases be an obstacle to international consensus on nonproliferation. Furthermore, enhancement of the nuclear nonproliferation regime may lead to a triple standard, since a way must be found to deal with the three undeclared nuclear powers, India, Pakistan, and Israel. Will they be treated as *de facto* nuclear states, or will they be asked to eliminate weapons they do not admit to having?

Proliferation occurs in the context of international conflict. China wanted nuclear weapons to counter those of the United States and the Soviet Union; India responded to China's weapon, and Pakistan to India's. The Islamic countries want to catch up with Israel. In the latter case, Israel's adversaries also have pursued chemical and probably biological weapons in part to try counter the Israeli nuclear advantage. Such countries might not be talked out of pursuing one kind of weapon of mass destruction unless they are convinced that their opponents will verifiably renounce not only that kind, but others as well. (In some cases, even that may not suffice: Israel seems unlikely to give up its nuclear weapons unless its general military security is assured.)

Weapons of mass destruction are sometimes expected to compensate for inferior conventional military power. This was the case for the United States and NATO during most of the Cold War.[4] Some countries vulnerable to threats of nuclear or conventional attack—for example, Germany, Japan, and South Korea—found it easier to forgo nuclear weapons because they could rely on the US nuclear deterrent umbrella. Lacking a comparable commitment, Israel developed its own nuclear deterrent against conventional attack by any or all of its Arab adversaries. Given the special dangers posed by weapons of mass destruction, it would probably be desirable to treat proliferation separately from other political and security issues. In the current regions of concern, however, such compartmentalization is unlikely to work. Agreements to forgo weapons of mass destruction may depend on complementary agreements to reduce perceived conventional military threats.

---

[4] The idea that Western superiority in conventional military technology—rather than US nuclear weapons—could counter Warsaw Pact numerical advantage was emphasized mainly in the later years of the Cold War, especially as discomfort with the idea of extended nuclear deterrence grew. Until the very end, the United States declined to follow the Soviet example (however disingenuous it might have been) of declaring that it would not be the first to use nuclear weapons.

Chapter 7

Toward Nuclear Disarmament and Global Security

Now that the Cold War is over, people expect deep cuts in military forces and spending. Instead, nuclear arsenals remain dangerously large, proliferation risks are neglected, and the global spread of advanced conventional weaponry continues unabated.

Up to now, hopes for a post–Cold War breakthrough have been disappointed. The five nuclear powers—the United States, Russia, China, France, and Britain—are *formally* committed to eliminate nuclear weapons, but none has presented ideas on the long-term future of nuclear weapons, much less a way to meet the NPT Article VI obligation to move in good faith toward the elimination of such weapons.

The picture is even more grim for cutbacks in conventional weapons and progress toward the NPT Article VI obligation for member nations to move toward general and complete disarmament. The five nuclear powers produce nearly all of the world's conventional weaponry. In the case of advanced combat aircraft, for example, they account for 99 percent of the systems now in service worldwide. In 1993, the United States alone was responsible for 75 percent of all international transfers of major conventional weapons. Thus these countries have not only vital interests in reducing regional military threats, but also a powerful means of doing so—that is, controlling their own arms exports. Yet they have made no serious effort to limit the international trade in conventional armaments. Similarly, three of the nuclear powers—the United States, Russia, and China—maintain the world's largest armies, in large part to deter and defend against wars with each other; yet they have made no effort to negotiate stabilizing reductions and restructuring of conventional forces, which would reduce the risks of war.[1]

Paradoxically, conditions have never been more favorable for major breakthroughs in the control of nuclear and conventional weapons.[2] For the first time in centuries, no conflict is brewing among the world's major powers. In fact, these countries are cooperating on some measures of arms control and peacekeeping. But there are opportunities for much more far-reaching cooperation to strengthen their own security and that of all other nations.

The following section looks at cooperative measures in the area of nuclear arms control and disarmament, which would greatly reduce the risk of nuclear war and greatly strengthen nonproliferation efforts. The discussion then turns to ways to reduce the risk of conventional war and to establish an effective world security system.

Eliminating the Danger of Nuclear War

In some areas of nuclear arms control, there has been important progress.[3] This progress includes the US-Soviet treaty eliminating intermediate-range ballistic missiles; the parallel US and Russian programs to withdraw most shorter-range tactical nuclear systems from operational deployment; deactivation and detargeting of US and Russian strategic nuclear weapons; and the two START treaties, START I, which went into effect in December 1994, and START II, which has not yet been ratified. There are good prospects for renewal of the Nonproliferation Treaty in some form, and reasonable prospects for conclusion of a treaty that will end all tests of nuclear warheads. A treaty ending the production of fissile material for weapons probably lies some years off.

---

[1] Reductions in conventional forces in Europe currently under way were negotiated before the dissolution of the Soviet Union and the Warsaw Pact and the unification of Germany. To date, there has been no serious consideration of new talks on the further cuts that might now be possible and desirable.
[2] Conditions are also promising for the control and even abolition of chemical and biological weapons, but measures aimed specifically at such systems, discussed in earlier chapters, are not elaborated further in this chapter.
[3] This section draws on Jonathan Dean, "The Final Stage of Nuclear Arms Control," *Washington Quarterly*, Fall 1994, which gives a more detailed analysis.

The potential test ban and fissile cutoff treaties are important not only because they meet conditions that the non-nuclear weapon NPT states have put forward for extending the NPT, but also because they would strengthen controls on existing nuclear arsenals by making it difficult to increase their size and to develop new nuclear warheads.

CONTINUING NUCLEAR DANGERS

These steps fall far short of what is needed to bring the risk of nuclear war to a minimum. Even the START treaties, if implemented, would leave the United States and Russia with very large arsenals of nuclear warheads on intercontinental missiles and aircraft—more than 3,000 each; and there is no agreement limiting the arsenals of Britain, France, or China. The current nonproliferation regime (the NPT and the export controls that augment it) is neither comprehensive nor fully effective. It has not prevented the worldwide spread of technical knowledge on how to construct nuclear weapons, nor the development of nuclear weapon know-how by South Africa, India, Pakistan, Israel, Iraq, and possibly North Korea, and to a lesser extent Argentina and Brazil. Nor has it put an end to the mounting stockpiles of weapon-usable plutonium produced for power reactors.

The most urgent dangers are those arising from Russia's nuclear arsenal, which combines large numbers and proliferation risks. The news from Russia in 1993 and 1994 was not good: near civil war and shelling of the Supreme Soviet in October 1993; a pronounced move to the nationalist right in the December 1993 elections; the collapse of the ruble in October 1994; and the Chechen disaster in December 1994, along with fighting in Moldova, Georgia, Azerbaijan, and Tajikistan. The membership of the Russian parliament may become still more nationalistic in the December 1995 elections, and Boris Yeltsin may be replaced by a more nationalistic opponent in the June 1996 presidential elections.

Indeed, the question of whether democratic institutions can strike enduring roots in Russia may remain open for another 20–30 years. The emergence of an authoritarian government that might use Russia's nuclear weapons as a basis for threats and pressures against nearby states will remain a possibility throughout this period. Economic hardship will continue. The rates of serious criminal activity and corruption among Russian officials, including military officers, are very high and growing. Numerous incidents, fortunately still small in scale, have illustrated the alarming possibility of "leakage" of warheads, fissile material, or nuclear components away from Russian government control through forcible seizure, theft, or illegal sale.

Similar problems may arise in China, where nuclear testing continues, the armed forces are expanding while the country enters a succession crisis, and the government is trying to limit the political impact of rapid but geographically uneven economic development. There is a real risk in China of regional frictions, factional struggles over control of nuclear weapons (today's symbol of government authority or legitimacy), and conflicts with neighboring states.

The wholehearted support of the non-nuclear weapon states is needed to operate the nonproliferation regime more effectively and to take the difficult steps needed to remedy its serious deficiencies. Yet such support may not be forthcoming, in large part because of dissatisfaction with failure of the nuclear weapon states to move more decisively toward eliminating their own nuclear arsenals.

The most urgent requirements of the situation are twofold: To cope more effectively with proliferation dangers, including the dangers of leakage from the Russian nuclear arsenal, and to guard against frictions among the nuclear weapon states leading to renewal of the nuclear arms race in a new form. To achieve these ends, the export controls and the verification of nonproduction of nuclear weapons must be greatly tightened. To eliminate the possibility that states can remain outside the regime, as North Korea did for a long time, the nonproliferation regime must be made fully comprehensive by bringing in the threshold states— Israel, India, and Pakistan. Finally, it is essential to remove a key incentive for the acquisition of nuclear weapons, by eliminating the possibility of surprise attack or threats based on possession of nuclear weapons by existing nuclear weapon states. It is not enough merely to call for action on these issues. A practical, comprehensive way to meet these requirements must be developed and governments must be persuaded to follow it.

Three key steps in the process must be, first, to get as many as possible of Russia's warheads and as much as possible of Russia's fissile material out of exclusive Russian control, with reciprocal US action as the incentive; second, to include Britain, France, and China and the three threshold nuclear weapon states in an arms control regime; and third, to induce all five declared nuclear weapon states to trade in a large part of their remaining arsenals in return for agreement by the non-nuclear states to radical improvements in the nonproliferation regime.

DEALING WITH RUSSIAN AND US NUCLEAR FORCES

In the long run, the nuclear powers must choose between having large nuclear arsenals and preventing others from having them. The Clinton administration seems to sense this trade-off, but is seeking to cope with the dangers of the Russian nuclear arsenal through two potentially conflicting programs: one maintains a nuclear deterrent against the contingency of Russian aggression, the other involves a cooperative program with Russia to prevent leakage from the Russian arsenal. If these two activities were explicitly linked—for example, if the United States and Russia agreed to reduce their deterrent stockpiles while at the same time making them leak proof—this approach might be sensible. But no comprehensive plan for nuclear weapon reductions and safeguarding has been developed; in fact, up to now the Clinton administration and the Russian government have both avoided it.

Even after START II, the United States and Russia will have nuclear arsenals ten-fold larger than those of China, France, or Britain, maintained on each side mainly against the contingency that the other misbehaves. The deployment and the doctrine underlying deployment of these large forces remain hostage to the future ups and downs of the US-Russian relationship. The result could be a smaller but still highly dangerous version of Cold War nuclear confrontation. Moreover, over the next several decades a posture of deterrence cannot prevent what may well be the most plausible nuclear threat to the United States and other nuclear weapon states—nuclear weapons anonymously smuggled into a number of cities and set off simultaneously.

The US and Russian governments' efforts to prevent loss or theft of Russian nuclear weapons lack comprehensive coverage, an agreed goal, and central direction. They are painfully slow, experimental, and partial. Public interest groups have pressed since the mid-1980s for a comprehensive, regular exchange of data on all warheads and fissile materials. In early 1995, ten years later, the possibility of a data exchange is still under discussion. There is also joint discussion of bilateral monitoring of warhead dismantling, but this measure, if implemented, would be experimental and would not cover all Russian assembly plants and storage sites.

The United States has agreed to buy 500 tons of HEU taken from dismantled Russian nuclear warheads. Unfortunately, there will be no real assurance that the material does come from Russian weapons, the program will extend over a 20-year period, it may cover less than half of Russian holdings, and there may never be effective monitoring of Russian stocks of weapon-grade plutonium.

Neither government sees this program as an example of a potential method of jointly reducing nuclear arsenals. Instead, it is considered primarily a means for the United States to help out on a Russian problem. The Clinton administration does have an innovative program to put fissile material that is not employed in bombs into IAEA-monitored storage, but it is not clear that Russia will take parallel action. In any event, the program will be wholly voluntary, with no future obligation that could make it a mechanism of disarmament.

START I went into effect in early December 1994. START II may be ratified by the US Senate, but ratification by the Russian Duma is likely to be difficult. Even if ratified, the START treaties are arms control agreements, not disarmament agreements. The treaties withdraw many strategic-range nuclear weapons from operational deployment, reducing the serious dangers of preemptive strike and accidental launch, which were the biggest threats of the Cold War period. The treaties also require the destruction of many launchers and delivery systems—silos, aircraft, and submarines. In addition, many tactical-range warheads withdrawn from deployment by the United States and Russia are being dismantled and some missiles are being destroyed. But the START accords, important as they are, serve largely to move the Cold War nuclear confrontation from field deployment to reserve status; they do not eliminate the confrontation. Under START, most US and Russian nuclear weapons (both strategic warheads and many missiles) are being not dismantled but stored; and even when the warheads are being dismantled, their fissile material is being stored.

The defense departments in both nations insist on maintaining a reserve of warheads for deployment if the other misbehaves. In sum, for the longer run, the START treaties allow the United States and Russia to maintain large reserves of warheads, fissile material, and fixed-base strategic missiles, over and above the vast arsenals which will be actively deployed after START II—reserves which could destroy both countries many times over.

REAL US AND RUSSIAN NUCLEAR DISARMAMENT
Genuine US-Russian nuclear disarmament would require three steps. First, the establishment of a comprehensive system of joint bilateral monitoring. In order to minimize the possibility of forcible seizure,

theft, or illegal sale, this system should cover all US and Russian stockpiles of warheads and fissile materials, plants for nuclear weapon assembly and dismantling, and plants that produce fissile materials. This monitoring can take place at current storage sites. The monitors would not have to know details of the weapons or fissile material at the site; they would merely assure that nothing was withdrawn from the premises without a previously agreed authorization. The monitors could be overpowered or asked to leave, but not without giving some form of warning to the international community.

Second, there should be a US-Russian agreement to dismantle *all* warheads withdrawn from operational deployment, whether by bilateral agreement or unilateral action; to transfer their *entire* fissile content to internationally-monitored storage; to produce no new warheads beyond replacements; and to cease production of fissile material for weapons, closing or monitoring the plants concerned. (Once an international treaty to end production of fissile material for weapons is agreed, it will replace the bilateral agreement.)

Third, missiles withdrawn from operational deployment should be destroyed (with limited, verified exceptions for space research and satellite launch), and production of missiles with a range over 100 km (except for the same purposes) should be banned. Destroying longer-range missiles and ending their production will establish a basis for a global regime to ban production of long-range ballistic missiles, and it will provide additional insurance against the possibility that warheads may be concealed to avoid very deep cuts in the arsenals.

Combined, these measures would form a process of "irreversible nuclear disarmament," the phrase used in 1994 by Presidents Clinton and Yeltsin to describe their long-term goal. The key action is to dismantle all warheads withdrawn from deployment and put their fissile material in bilaterally or internationally monitored storage (or a combination of the two). This is the central dynamic of irreversible nuclear disarmament; anything less is arms control. Nuclear disarmament requires getting the retired fissile material for weapons out of the hands of individual nuclear weapon states (beyond their power to use in new or refashioned weapons) and stopping the production of new material. When these steps have been taken, the United States and Russia will at last be honoring the spirit and the letter of their NPT obligation to move toward nuclear disarmament.

NEUTRALIZING NUCLEAR WEAPONS

Even if the two governments agree on a process of verified, irreversible reduction in nuclear weapons and the United States and Russia cut back to 1,000 or even 500 deployed warheads, the whole range of dangers from the Russian arsenal will remain. This means decades of worry in other countries about Russia's political instability and its potential nuclear consequences, and also about China's nuclear capabilities.

What is needed to cope with these risks and gain broad international political support for tightening the nonproliferation regime is a program to "neutralize" the nuclear arsenals of the five nuclear powers. In this context, neutralization means reducing nuclear arsenals to a minimum and making it very difficult to use the remaining weapons.

The first and most urgent step toward the longer-term goal of neutralizing all nuclear weapons is to begin with the reciprocal monitoring and irreversible build-down of US and Russian arsenals, as described above. Next, the same measures and techniques must be applied to the arsenals of France, Britain and China. Indeed, once the United States and Russia agree to dismantle their decommissioned warheads and transfer the withdrawn fissile material to bilaterally or internationally monitored storage, they will be strongly motivated to bring the remaining nuclear weapon states into the same arrangement.

As suggested by many experts, the United States and Russia might begin by reducing their nuclear arsenals to 500–1,000 warheads each. Then they would join with Britain, France, and China in a series of further reductions, accompanied by other steps described above: multilateral monitoring of stored warheads and fissile material; the dismantling of all decommissioned warheads and missiles; the transfer of all fissile material from the warheads to internationally-supervised custody; and the establishment of a zero alert status for the weapons that are still deployed (that is, detargeting and separating warheads from delivery systems to the extent possible, to create a margin of time before they can be used).

How far should irreversible reductions go?

The public and the governments of non-nuclear states throughout the world should continue to call for the complete elimination of nuclear weapons even though for now, the nuclear powers are not likely to seriously consider a time-specified commitment to abolish their nuclear arsenals. Attitudes in the nuclear weapon states may change, but probably not until there is a functioning world security system. This goal, discussed below, will take decades to achieve.

In the interim, a great deal can be done to reduce the dangers of the nuclear weapons that remain. The best way to proceed is to begin with a concept of the *end point* for negotiated nuclear weapon reductions that involves very deep cuts, yet has a real prospect of eventual acceptance by the nuclear powers. The end point must offer the nuclear powers greater security than they would derive from maintaining nuclear deterrence at higher levels. In other words, it must reduce the dangers from other nuclear powers and from possible proliferants. In addition, to persuade non-nuclear states to accept far-reaching measures to tighten the nonproliferation regime, the end point must show substantial progress toward the goal of complete nuclear disarmament.

The negotiated neutralization of nuclear weapons could come close to nuclear disarmament without posing new dangers of low-level vulnerability and instability if there were an agreement of the following kind: the five nuclear powers would reduce their total arsenals to, say, 200 warheads each; they would separate the remaining ground-based warheads from their delivery systems; and they would permit multilateral monitoring of the warheads and delivery systems on their territory. Because missile-equipped submarines would be difficult to constrain under such a regime, each nuclear weapon state would be permitted no more than two missile-equipped submarines with a total of no more than 6–8 single-warhead missiles. The proposed 200-warhead level is about equal to the current size of the smallest declared nuclear arsenal (that of Britain). The equal level for all five countries will probably be needed to gain China's agreement.

The nuclear powers would commit themselves to dismantle their warheads as they move toward the 200-warhead level and to place all fissile material from these weapons (and any other stocks of fissile material) under international monitoring.

At this stage, the threshold nuclear states—Israel, India, and Pakistan—would be asked to choose between relinquishing their nuclear weapon materials or placing them in multilaterally-monitored storage under the conditions that would apply to the acknowledged nuclear powers. They would have access to their material and warheads, but could not remove them from storage without warning the international monitors; and they would be subject to the same verification measures that apply to other participants.

One precondition for this final stage of nuclear arms control would be the successful implementation of a verifiable treaty ending the production of fissile material for weapons—a treaty in which the threshold nuclear weapon states would be expected to participate. Another prerequisite is the strengthening of the IAEA and its safeguard capabilities. Among other things, NPT states must be required to report to the IAEA all sales of nuclear-related materials listed by the IAEA and to permit "anywhere-anytime" special inspections by the IAEA as well as its use of remote air and water sensors. Also needed is a decision by the members of the UN Security Council to act jointly against states that reject international safeguards over their nuclear capacity: No country can be allowed to stay outside this regime because the advantages of noncompliance (that is, retaining the capability to build nuclear weapons) are too great. While committing themselves to a policy of no-first-use of their nuclear weapons, the five nuclear powers would need to support joint action under UN Security Council auspices against any state or group threatening to initiate use of nuclear weapons.

The regime would also require a halt in the use of plutonium as fuel for nuclear-energy reactors. Since plutonium produced for power reactions can be used to manufacture nuclear weapons, the nuclear weapon states will not agree to reduce their weapons to very low levels while plutonium production continues. Plutonium can be replaced by low-enriched uranium, which is in plentiful supply.

Under the neutralization approach, the owning countries could withdraw their nuclear warheads from monitored storage in the event of an acute national emergency (as determined by the owner) or at the request of the UN Security Council. The monitoring regime would not be expected to prevent unauthorized withdrawal, but only to warn other nations if the monitors were ignored, removed, or forcibly overcome.

This approach does not eliminate the risk of concealed weapons. Part of the answer to this potential problem is deep dispersed storage, possibly with ground-based anti-aircraft and missile defenses to protect authorized arsenals against a small-scale attack made with previously concealed weapons. In addition, initially, each declared nuclear weapon state could retain two missile-equipped submarines. Their 6-8 warheads would be too few to destroy a nation, but enough to deter a counter-force nuclear attack employing previously concealed weapons.

In later stages of the neutralization process, even more far-reaching steps might be taken. For example, missile-equipped submarines might be banned, so that no nuclear weapons could be used at short notice. Eventually, all nuclear warheads and delivery vehicles might be dismantled, leaving the nuclear powers with only monitored stocks of fissile material.

In sum, the key components of this plan for a final stage of nuclear arms control are a fissile cut-off, drastic negotiated cuts in warheads and missiles, obligatory dismantling of decommissioned warheads and missiles, and obligatory transfer of the fissile material from decommissioned warheads and stored unweaponized stocks to internationally monitored storage. Each of these steps is feasible, and so is the whole program. The crucial first step in this process is for the United States and Russia to agree to dismantle all warheads withdrawn from operational deployment and put their fissile material in monitored storage.

The changes outlined here would eliminate the risk of large-scale nuclear attack without warning; drastically reduce the possibility of any use of nuclear weapons or secret development of nuclear weapon capability; and eliminate the threatened use of nuclear weapons as an instrument of coercion. If nuclear weapons were neutralized in this manner, they would cease to be a major factor in international security or international politics. Conditions would be established in which the total abolition of nuclear weapons might become feasible, that is, the nonproliferation regime could be further strengthened and the task of building an effective global security system could proceed.

Cooperating for Global Security

Yet to bear fruit is the most stunning effect of the Cold War's end: the opportunity for the United States, Russia, and other major military powers to cooperate fully in efforts to provide for their own security and global security. Now that they are no longer divided by unbridgeable differences in political and cultural values, the major powers could undertake efforts to limit armaments in ways that used to be unthinkable. By minimizing the risk of major conventional war, such efforts would reduce the incentives for the spread of weapons of mass destruction. They would also strengthen international norms against the use of force as a tool of policy (except for deterrence of and defense against the use of force by others) and permit deep cuts in military spending.

In the wake of the Cold War, the security concerns of the world's militarily strongest nations are largely shared. At present there is virtually no risk of a major war involving two or more of the world's military and economic "great powers," that is, the five nuclear powers plus Japan and Germany. For the longer term, the top security concern of the great powers is to keep that risk very low. Several cooperative arms control measures could help in this task. For example, mutually agreed reductions in the still-large standing conventional forces of these nations, along with defense-oriented changes in force structure and military tactics, would eliminate the capability for a massive surprise attack and strengthen confidence in the peace. If cutbacks in standing forces were combined with steps to "mothball" production lines for major offense-capable weapon systems, the combined measures would place steep economic and political hurdles in the path of aggressively-oriented rearmament by a future authoritarian leader. These measures to reduce fears of near-term and longer-term threats would permit deep cuts in military spending, and they would facilitate the steps discussed earlier to neutralize nuclear weapons.

The major concern of the most heavily armed regional military powers (and their less heavily armed neighbors), and the second most acute security concern of the great powers, involves threats of major regional war and the linked risks of proliferation of weapons of mass destruction. Here, too, a cooperative approach to security could reduce perceived threats, build confidence in the peace, facilitate diplomatic efforts to resolve conflicts, save scarce resources, and reduce or even eliminate the incentives for proliferation. Regional arms control efforts should focus on the same confidence-building measures proposed for the great powers: reductions in armed forces, defense-oriented restructuring of forces and tactics, and cutbacks in programs to build or strengthen arms-producing industries.

Regional arms control agreements would lead to a further dramatic reduction in the already greatly reduced Third World demand for imports of major weapons. Today, the arms producing nations are competing fiercely to sell weapons to Third World nations. In general, 70-80 percent of such sales go to handful of key players in regional conflicts, including the main candidates for nuclear proliferation: North Korea and, potentially, South Korea, Iran, Israel, and Iraq (if the arms and oil embargoes were dropped), and India and Pakistan.[4] Even though regional conventional arms races increase incentives for proliferation,

---

[4] Major weapon importers which are not likely nuclear proliferants are China (already a nuclear power), Taiwan, Saudi Arabia, Egypt, Turkey, and Greece.

commercial interests and industrial base issues are taking precedence over the proliferation problem in the policies of the great powers.

Coordinated arms control measures aimed at enhancing both great power security and global security would include regional and global-scope conventional reductions and restructuring, accompanied by cutbacks in (or a moratorium on) arms production and trade. Such a package would require an entirely new approach to preserving the defense industrial base. Instead of keeping industrial plant and know-how alive by procuring weapons not needed for national defense or by exporting weapons to Third World nations in conflict, the arms producers would need to develop a set of new techniques hitherto used only rarely. These involve putting production requirements and processes on videotape, using simulators to preserve or hone skills, and possibly establishing a new "industrial reserve corps" made up of engineers and assembly line workers.

Cooperative arms control measures to build confidence in the peace would create a breathing space, a period in which military threats do not change or appear unexpectedly on the radar screen. That quiet period would facilitate the development of a more comprehensive and lasting global security system. Such a system might include guidelines for defensively-oriented conventional forces; increased reliance on multilateral forces under UN (or other nonpartisan) auspices to deter and defend against aggression; the creation of a global verification, monitoring, and reconnaissance system, whose findings would be available to all governments (and, in many cases, to the public); and, last but not least, guidelines for the international community's use of military, diplomatic, and economic means to deter or reverse international aggression and to prevent or end genocide in bloody internal conflicts.

Talks on cooperative arms control measures and on possible elements of a global security system are not yet on the international agenda. The reason is not that such talks are premature, but that old thinking and vested interests still dominate the agenda. Increased public awareness, concern, and commotion could change that.

Appendix

14

Table 1: Weapon Agents of Mass Destruction[1]

Type of weapon agent	Examples	Mechanism	Effects on human beings
Nuclear: fission and fusion	Hiroshima fission bomb = 12.5 kt (1 kt = 1,000 tons TNT); fusion bomb, e.g., largest U.S. test = 17 Mt (1 Mt = 1,000,000 tons TNT)	Blast (overpressure)	Bleeding and rupture; violent displacement; blows or crushing by debris
		Thermal radiation	Flash burns, blinding, burning or suffocation from building fires
		Nuclear radiation (immediate)	Vomiting, diarrhea, fever, bleeding, infection, circulatory failure, respiratory failure, brain swelling
		Nuclear radiation (delayed effects and fallout effects)	Above effects at high doses; contact burns, cataracts, leukemia, other cancers, birth defects at lower doses
Biological: viruses	Venezuelan equine encephalitis	Inhaled or ingested infectious diseases	A variety of debilitating or potentially fatal illnesses
bacteria	Anthrax, brucellosis, plague	(same)	(same)
rickettsiae	Q fever, typhus	(same)	(same)

Toxins:[2]	Botulin, ricin, animal venoms	Inhaled or ingested poisons	A variety of toxic effects, often fatal
Chemical: Blistering (Vesicants)	Mustard, lewisite	Skin and tissue destruction on contact or inhalation	Skin blistering, blindness, potentially fatal lung damage
Choking	Chlorine, Phosgene, PFIB	Lung damage on inhalation	Fluid build-up leading to fatal choking
Blood	Cyanogen chloride, hydrogen cyanide	Blocking of blood oxygen on inhalation	Anoxia (severe oxygen starvation of body tissues)
Nerve	Tabun (GA), Sarin (GB), Soman (GD), GF, VX	Nervous system disruption on contact or inhalation	Convulsions, paralysis leading to death

1 Some chemical and biological agents may cause irritation, illness, or behavior changes, but may not normally be fatal; weapons using these agents may incapacitate people for hours, days or weeks, but cannot be accurately said to inflict mass destruction. Other agents can destroy livestock or crops, having great potential for economic warfare but (except for the possibility of causing mass starvation) not leading immediately to widespread human injury.

2 Toxins are nonliving, poisonous chemicals, first produced in biological processes. It was therefore reasonable to consider them to be biological weapons, and they are covered in the international treaty banning biological weapons. However, as toxic chemical (nonliving) substances, they are also categorized as "chemical" weapon agents—and they are so considered in the Chemical Weapons Convention banning chemical weapons.

Table 2: Steps to Produce and Deploy Nuclear Weapons

Acquisition of nuclear weapon materials

- Mining of uranium-bearing ore
- Milling to extract uranium concentrate in the form of "yellowcake" (U_3O_8) or other uranates[a]
- Chemical processing to convert yellowcake into useful compounds (such as UO_2, UF_6, UF_4, UCl_4)

—Uranium-235 based weapons:

- Enrichment of uranium to high levels of uranium-235 (most often carried out using uranium hexafluoride, UF_6, or other uranium compounds)
- Conversion of enriched uranium product to uranium metal

—Plutonium-based weapons:

- Uranium fuel fabrication in the form of metal or oxide (using alloys, ceramics, zircalloy or aluminum cladding, etc.)
- Reactor construction and operation (typically requiring a graphite or heavy-water moderator[b], unless enriched uranium fuel were available)
- Reprocessing of spent fuel to extract plutonium product
- Conversion of plutonium product to plutonium metal

Weapon fabrication (plutonium or uranium weapons)

- Design and fabrication of fissile core
- Design and fabrication of nonnuclear components (chemical explosives, detonator, fuze, neutron initiator, reflector, etc.)
- Weapon assembly

Weapon testing and deployment

- Physics tests (hydrodynamic, hydronuclear, or nuclear—see text)
- Development of delivery system and integration with warhead
- Weapon transport and storage
- Possible development of doctrine and training for use

[a] U_3O_8 can also be purchased on the international market; transfers to or from NPT parties with safeguards agreements in force must be reported to the IAEA, but do not require inspections.

[b] The moderator in a nuclear reactor slows down the neutrons produced in fission reactions so that they can more efficiently induce subsequent fission reactions. Heavy-water and ultra-pure graphite are effective neutron moderators having very low neutron absorption, thus permitting reactors to operate on natural uranium.

Table 3: U.S. Unilateral Proliferation-Related Export Control Legislation[1]

Legislation, Regulation, or Executive Order	Description or Comment
Atomic Energy Act of 1954 (as amended)	Sets guidelines for dissemination and restriction of data relating to nuclear weapons.
	Provides statutory framework for export controls on nuclear trade.
Nuclear Non-Proliferation Act of 1978	Tightens export controls by requiring IAEA full-scope safeguards as a condition for exports of nuclear fuel and reactors.
	Seeks to establish U.S. as reliable supplier for nuclear reactors and fuels to nations adhering to nonproliferation policies.
	Seeks to strengthen international controls over transfer and use of nuclear materials and technology.
	Directs the President to seek agreement from all exporting nations to require recipients of nuclear technology and materials to accept International Atomic Energy Agency (IAEA) "full-scope" safeguards on all peaceful nuclear activities.
	Further specifies legal guidelines for regulation of nuclear commerce and technical assistance.
	Directs the President to publish procedures for the Commerce Department to control U.S. exports of "dual-use" items that could be used for nuclear explosives.
	Defines jurisdiction of Departments of State, Energy, Defense, and Arms Control and Disarmament Agency over nuclear exports.

Table 3 (Continued)

Legislation, Regulation, or Executive Order	Description or Comment
Export Administration Act of 1979 and Executive Order 12735 (Nov. 16, 1990) on Chemical and Biological Weapons Proliferation	Commerce Department, after consulting with State and Defense, issues Export Administration Regulations; its Bureau of Export Administration administers export licenses on controlled commodities (including nuclear, chemical, or biological weapons-related or missile-related, as well as other items controlled for national security or foreign policy purposes). Authority extends primarily over dual-use goods. EAA of 1979, the primary authority for U.S. export controls, expired Sept. 30, 1990; President Bush vetoed successor act but extended export control authority by executive order under emergency power (conferred by the International Emergency Economic Powers Act of 1977). In 1992 Congress passed an interim renewal of the 1979 Act.
Chemical and Biological Weapons Control and Warfare Elimination Act of 1991	Amended EAA to require Secretary of Commerce to establish and maintain "a list of goods and technology that would directly and substantially assist a foreign government or group in acquiring the capability to develop, produce, stockpile, or deliver chemical or biological weapons" if licensing them would be effective, and then keep a list of countries for which exporters must obtain validated export licenses.
Arms Export Control Act of 1976	Authorizes State Department (through its Center for Defense Trade) to control by licenses items (including chemical and biological warfare agents and missiles) covered by International Traffic in Arms Regulations and U.S. Munitions List. In contrast to Export Administration Regulations (above), authority of this act extends mainly over sales of conventional weapons and weapon components.

[1] Many other laws address nonproliferation issues; this list only covers the major ones.

Table 4: Current Multilateral Proliferation-Related Export Control Agreements

Agreement	Provisions or Comment
Treaty on the Non-Proliferation of Nuclear Weapons (NPT) (entered into force Mar. 5, 1970)	Nuclear weapon state parties (now including China, France, Russia, United Kingdom and United States) agree not to transfer nuclear devices to any recipient, nor to assist any non-nuclear-weapon State to make or acquire them. All state parties agree not to transfer nuclear materials or related equipment to any non-nuclear-weapon state unless the latter will accept International Atomic Energy Agency safeguards (monitoring) over the materials.
Nuclear Suppliers' Guidelines: Nuclear Exporters Committee (Zangger Committee) and London Suppliers Group (London Club)	To strengthen and better implement NPT export restrictions, seven NPT members who were major nuclear suppliers (the Zangger Committee) agreed informally in 1971 on a list of nuclear technology items, the transfer of which would trigger application of IAEA safeguards to ensure that the items were not used to develop nuclear explosives. Forming the "London Club," in 1976, 8 more nuclear supplier nations (including France, not then an NPT member) joined those on the Zangger Committee and agreed on a set of Nuclear Suppliers' Guidelines, under which "trigger list" exports would further require physical security for transferred items, acceptance of safeguards on facilities replicated from London Club member designs, and prohibitions against retransfer of items to third parties; suppliers also agreed to "exercise restraint" in transfer of nuclear-sensitive facilities, technologies, and weapons-usable materials. Total of 27 nuclear suppliers agreed in April 1992 to an additional list of 65 categories of dual-use items to be controlled. Participating nations have adapted these controls voluntarily. There is no international mechanism for monitoring and enforcement, but a Japanese-administered secretariat in Vienna is now overseeing the application of the dual-use guidelines.
Australia Group	Group of industrialized nations agreed in 1984 to establish national controls on chemical weapon agents and precursor chemicals that could be used to make them. Group, then with 22 members, agreed in March 1992 to add to the control list organisms, toxins, and equipment that might be used to make biological weapons. Has no formal coordination, monitoring, or enforcement, but does have informal agreements to share intelligence and notice of export denials. Eleven other states apply some or all Australia group standards.

Table 4 (Continued)

Agreement	Provisions or Comment
Missile Technology Control Regime (MTCR)	Group of supplier nations agreed in 1987 not to transfer complete rocket systems or subsystems, or production facilities for them. Group now consists of 23 states, plus 2 "partners"; other states, including Argentina, Israel, Russia, and China, have separately promised United States that they will abide by MTCR constraints. Members also agree to restrain exports of other components, material, or technology that would be useful in missile production. Applies to missiles of range over 300 km; also applies to *any* missiles which the member government judges to be intended for use with weapons of mass destruction. Agreement is subject to no formal coordination, monitoring, or enforcement.
Coordinating Committee on Multilateral Export Controls, (CoCom)	Group of U.S. allies in 1949 agreed not to export listed items (including some related to missiles and weapons of mass destruction) to Communist countries. Controls have been relaxed after collapse of the Soviet bloc. CoCom is unique among supplier agreements in attempting to establish common standards of enforcement of national export controls among the members; however, it is ill-suited to control proliferation-sensitive technology because the very states that were its targets—Communist and former-Communist states—would have to be members of any nonproliferation export control regime. CoCom might serve as model for other agreements.[1]
U.S.-foreign bilateral arrangements	As noted above, in some cases the United States obtains bilateral agreement with individual nations to abide by supplier group restraints. State Department also issues diplomatic demarches, urging individual foreign governments to impose controls on specific exports of concern discovered by the United States.

Table 5: Legislative Bases of U.S. Sanctions Against Suppliers

Law	Description or Comment
Atomic Energy Act	Requires cutoff of nuclear cooperation with states that transfer U.S.-supplied nuclear materials or technology without U.S. permission.
	Requires cutoff of nuclear cooperation with nuclear-weapon states that assist, encourage, or induce a non-nuclear-weapon state to engage in activities that involve nuclear materials and are significant for the making or acquisition of a nuclear explosive device.
Glenn (1977) and Symington (1977) amendments (sections 669 and 670) to Foreign Assistance Act of 1961 (FAA)	Require President (unless he issues waiver) to cut off economic and military aid to countries that supply the wherewithal for enriching uranium or extracting plutonium from spent nuclear fuel when all the recipient's nuclear facilities are not under IAEA safeguards.
Chemical and Biological Weapons Control and Warfare Elimination Act of 1991	Requires President (unless he issues waiver) to deny U.S. Government procurement or any U.S. imports from 'foreign persons' (individuals or firms) knowingly and materially contributing to chemical or biological weapons proliferation through the export of goods or technologies either covered by the Act, or that would be covered by the Act if they were produced in the United States.
Missile Technology Control Act, 1990 (Title XVII of the FY 1991 National Defense Authorization Act, which added a chapter to the Arms Export Control Act and sections to the Export Administration Act of 1979)	Denies U.S. Government contracts or export licenses to U.S. or foreign persons who improperly export missiles or major components;
	Denies U.S. Government missile-related contracts or export licenses to those who improperly export missile components, materials, or test and production equipment;
	Provides for Presidential waivers of sanctions.
Iran-Iraq Nonproliferation Act of 1992 (A section of the FY 1993 Defense Authorization Act)	Extends sanctions to Iran that already apply to Iraq: a variety of sanctions against individuals, companies, and countries who knowingly assist Iran or Iraq to acquire weapons of mass destructionn.

Table 6: Legislative Bases of U.S. Sanctions Against Proliferant Countries

Law	Description or Comment
Nuclear Non-Proliferation Act of 1978 amendment to the Atomic Energy Act	Termination of nuclear exports if nation: • detonates a nuclear explosive device, • terminates or abrogates IAEA safeguards, • violates an IAEA safeguards agreement, • engages in activities involving nuclear materials and having direct significance for manufacture or acquisition of a nuclear explosive device. Prohibits sales of nuclear reactors and fuel to non-nuclear-weapon states that do not accept IAEA full-scope safeguards on all their nuclear installations.
Glenn-Symington amendments to Foreign Assistance Act (FAA), 1976 and 1977	Cutoff of military and economic assistance to nations: • receiving wherewithal for enriching uranium or reprocessing plutonium, unless all such facilities and materials are placed under IAEA safeguards, • receiving a nuclear explosive device, or • detonating a nuclear explosive device.
Solarz Amendment to FAA, 1985	Requires President (unless he issues waiver) to cut off aid to any country that illegally exports, or attempts to export, from the United States nuclear wherewithal that would "contribute significantly" to the ability of a country to construct a nuclear device.
Pressler Amendment to the FAA, 1985	In the 1980s, Presidents Reagan and Bush waived (as allowed by congressional amendments to the Act) the requirements of the Foreign Assistance Act to cut off aid to Pakistan because of its nuclear weapons program; In 1985, Congress added an amendment requiring the President to cut off aid to Pakistan unless he declared in writing that "Pakistan does not possess a nuclear explosive device and that the proposed U.S. assistance program will reduce significantly the risk that . . . [it will]"; in 1990, the President stopped such certifications, and aid stopped (although commercial military sales continued).
Chemical and Biological Weapons Control and Warfare Elimination Act of 1991	Requires President, on request of Chairman of House Foreign Affairs Committee or Senate Foreign Relations Committee, to report whether a specified government has used chemical or biological weapons; If use determined, mandates sanctions including: foreign aid cutoff, arms sales and military financing cutoff, cutoff of U.S. Government credit or other financial aid, cutoff of exports of any controlled national security goods and technology; If, within 3 months, President does not certify that country has ceased using the weapons, provided assurance that it will refrain in the future, and allowed outside inspections, additional sanctions are at least three of the following: U.S. opposition to multilateral financial or technical aid, prohibition of U.S. bank loans, ban on all exports (except agricultural), ban on imports originating in the country, downgrading of diplomatic relations, suspension of aviation rights; Presidential waivers of the sanctions are possible.

Glossary and Acronyms

Australia Group An export control regime devoted to preventing the transfer of chemical and biological weapon materials and technology to nations of proliferation concern.

ballistic missile A rocket-powered delivery vehicle that has some form of guidance system, and that travels a large portion of its flight in a ballistic (free-fall) trajectory.

BTW Biological or toxin warfare.

BWC Biological Weapon Convention. Formal title: Convention on the Prohibition of the Development, Production, and Stockpiling of Bacteriological (Biological) and Toxin Weapons and on Their Destruction.

Conference on Disarmament A Geneva-based, 37-nation forum under UN auspices devoted to discussing arms control and disarmament measures. Meets 24 weeks a year.

cruise missile An unmanned, self-propelled vehicle that sustains flight through the use of aerodynamic lift over most of its flight path and that is intended as a weapon-delivery vehicle.

CTB Comprehensive test ban; under negotiation at the Conference on Disarmament.

CWC Chemical Weapon Convention. Formal title: Convention on the Prohibition of the Development, Production, Stockpiling, and Use of Chemical Weapons and on Their Destruction.

delivery vehicle The component of a nuclear weapon system that transports a nuclear device to its target.

dual-use technology A technology with both military and civilian applications.

fissile material The essential fuel of nuclear weapons and nuclear reactors. Typically the term "fissile material" refers to highly enriched uranium (HEU), low-enriched uranium (LEU), or plutonium.

force de frappe French nuclear weapon force.

GPS Global Positioning System. A group of satellites that allow an individual or vehicle equipped with a GPS receiver to navigate with great precision.

HEU Highly enriched uranium. Uranium that contains the isotope U-235 in a concentration greater than 20 percent. Concentrations of 90 percent U-235 or higher are generally required for nuclear weapons and are called weapon-grade.

IAEA International Atomic Energy Agency. A UN organization founded in 1956 to promote peaceful uses of nuclear technology, prevent the diversion of safeguarded nuclear materials, and maintain health and safety standards for the nuclear industry and the environment. All non-nuclear weapon states party to the nuclear Nonproliferation Treaty must accept IAEA safeguards.

LEU Low-enriched uranium. Uranium that contains the isotope U-235 in concentrations less than 20 percent, but greater than the naturally occurring value of 0.7 percent; usually 2–5 percent.

MTCR Missile Technology Control Regime. An export control regime devoted to preventing the transfer of missile technology to nations of proliferation concern.

NPT Nuclear Nonproliferation Treaty. Formal title: Treaty on the Nonproliferation of Nuclear Weapons.

NSA Negative security assurance. An assurance offered by nuclear weapon states that they will not use or threaten to use nuclear weapons against non-nuclear weapon states.

NSG Nuclear Suppliers Group. A group of 28 nations that develops voluntary restrictions on nuclear material and technology transfers.

Nuclear weapon state One of the five nations permitted by the nuclear Nonproliferation Treaty to possess nuclear weapons: China, France, Russia, the United Kingdom, and the United States.

PALs Permissive action links. Locks that prevent the unauthorized use of nuclear weapons.

plutonium reprocessing The process of separating plutonium from irradiated uranium.

Scud missiles Commonly exported short-range ballistic missiles, originally produced in Russia, but now produced in several nations.

START I Strategic Arms Reduction Treaty. Formal title: Treaty Between the United States of America and the Union of Soviet Socialist Republics on the Reduction and Limitation of Strategic Offensive Arms. The treaty calls for reductions in the number of deployed strategic nuclear weapons in the United States and the former Soviet Union.

START II Follow-on agreement to START I. Formal title: Treaty Between the United States of America and the Russian Federation on Further Reduction and Limitation of Strategic Offensive Arms.

uranium enrichment The process of increasing the concentration of the isotope U-235 from its 0.7 percent concentration in natural uranium ore.

warhead The nuclear explosive component of a missile-based nuclear weapon system.

Further Reading

For the reader's convenience, this list contains sources used in this book's footnotes as well as additional valuable resources. Some of the items include a chapter reference to this book for readers interested in particular topics, while other items cover a broader range of nonproliferation issues and therefore have no specific chapter reference.

Allison, Graham, Ashton Carter, Steven Miller, and Philip Zelikow, *Cooperative Denuclearization: From Pledges to Deeds*, Cambridge, MA: Center for Science and International Affairs, Harvard University, January 1993.

Arms Control Reporter (monthly), Cambridge, MA: Institute for Defense and Disarmament Studies.

Arms Control Today (monthly), Washington, DC: Arms Control Association.

Burrows, William and Robert Windrem, *Critical Mass: The Dangerous Race for Superweapons in a Fragmenting World*, New York: Simon and Schuster, 1994. (Chapter 2)

Campbell, Kurt, Ashton Carter, Steven Miller, and Charles Zraket, *Soviet Nuclear Fission: Control of the Nuclear Arsenal in a Disintegrating Soviet Union*, Cambridge, MA: Center for Science and International Affairs, Harvard University, November 1991. (Chapter 2)

Carter, Ashton B., William J. Perry, and John D. Steinbruner, *A New Concept of Cooperative Security*, Washington, DC: Brookings Institution, 1992.

Cohen, Jonathan and Andrew Peach, *IDDS Almanac 1994: World Combat Aircraft Holdings, Production, and Trade*, Cambridge, MA: Institute for Defense and Disarmament Studies, 1994. (Chapter 2)

Dean, Jonathan, "The Final Stage of Nuclear Arms Control," *The Washington Quarterly*, Fall 1994. (Chapter 7)

Ellsberg, Daniel, "Manhattan Project II: To End the Threat of Nuclear War," *Harvard Journal of World Affairs*, Summer 1992. (Chapter 2)

Forsberg, Randall, "Creating a Cooperative Security System, *Boston Review*, Vol. XVII, No. 2 (November-December 1992), pp. 7-10. (Available in an IDDS reprint, which includes comments by Hayward Alker, Jr, Jonathan Dean, Carl Kaysen, Joanne Landy, Steven Miller, and Stephen Van Evera.) (Chapters 1 and 7)

Forsberg, Randall, ed., *The Arms Production Dilemma: Contraction and Restraint in the World Combat Aircraft Industry*, Cambridge, MA: The MIT Press, 1994. (Chapters 1 and 7)

Glasstone, Samuel and Philip J. Dolan, eds., *The Effect of Nuclear Weapons*, Washington, DC: US Departments of Defense and Energy, 1977. (Chapters 2 and 3)

Harrison, Selig, "Zero Nuclear Weapons. Zero." *New York Times*, February 15, 1995. (Chapter 2)

Hersh, Seymour, "On the Nuclear Edge," *The New Yorker*, March 29, 1993. (On the Indian-Pakistani nuclear faceoff.) (Chapter 2)

Jehl, Douglas, "Who Armed Iraq? Answers the West Didn't Want to Hear," *New York Times*, July 18, 1993. (Chapters 2 and 5)

Milhollin, Gary, "Licensing Mass Destruction: US Exports to Iraq, 1985-1990," manuscript, Wisconsin Project on Nuclear Arms Control, June 1991. (Chapters 2 and 6)

Milhollin, Gary, "The Iraqi Bomb," *The New Yorker*, February 1, 1993. (Chapter 2)

Natural Resources Defense Council, *Nuclear Weapons Databook*, Vols. I–V, 1984–1994. (Chapters 2 and 3)

The Nonproliferation Review (published three times per year), Monterey, CA: Monterey Institute of International Studies.

Office of Technology Assessment, US Congress, *Technology Against Terrorism: Structuring Security*, OTA-ISC-511, Washington, DC: US Government Printing Office, January 1992. (Chapter 2)

Office of Technology Assessment, US Congress, *The Chemical Weapons Convention: Effects on the US Chemical Industry*, OTA-BP-ISC-106, Washington, DC: US Government Printing Office, August 1993. Chapters 4 and 5)

Office of Technology Assessment, US Congress, *Proliferation of Weapons of Mass Destruction: Assessing the Risks*, OTA-ISC-559, Washington, DC: US Government Printing Office, August 1993.

Office of Technology Assessment, US Congress, *Technologies Underlying Weapons of Mass Destruction*, Washington, DC: US Government Printing Office, December 1993.

Office of Technology Assessment, US Congress, *Export Controls and Nonproliferation Policy*, Washington, DC: US Government Printing Office, May 1994. (Chapter 5)

Potter, William and Harlan Jencks, *The International Missile Bazaar: The New Suppliers' Network*, Boulder, CO: Westview Press, 1994. (Chapters 2 and 5)

Redick, John, "Argentina-Brazil Nuclear Non-Proliferation Initiatives," Programme for Promoting Nuclear Non-Proliferation, January 1994. (Chapters 2 and 4)

Rhodes, Richard, *The Making of the Atomic Bomb*, New York: Simon and Schuster, 1986. (Chapter 3)

Spector, Leonard, with Jacqueline Smith, *Nuclear Ambitions: The Spread of Nuclear Weapons 1989-1990*, The Carnegie Endowment for International Peace, Boulder, CO: Westview Press, 1990. (Chapter 2)

Spector, Leonard and Virginia Foran, *Preventing Weapons Proliferation: Should the Regimes Be Combined?*, Muscatine, IA: The Stanley Foundation, 1992. (Chapter 5)

Thorne, Carlton, "The Nuclear Suppliers Group: A Major Success Story Gone Unnoticed," *Director's Series on Proliferation*, Lawrence Livermore National Laboratory, January 5, 1994. (Chapter 5)

Tsipis, Kosta, *Arsenal: Understanding Weapons in the Nuclear Age*, New York: Simon and Schuster, 1983.

Turco, R.P, O.B. Toon, T.P. Ackerman, J.B. Pollack, and Carl Sagan, "Nuclear Winter: Global Consequences of Multiple Nuclear Explosions," *Science*, December 23, 1983. (Chapter 2)

US Arms Control and Disarmament Agency (ACDA), *Arms Control and Disarmament Agreements: Texts and Histories of the Negotiations*, sixth edition, Washington, DC: ACDA, 1990.

US National Academy of Sciences and Russian Academy of Sciences, "Dual Use Technologies and Export Administration in the Post Cold War Era," National Academy of Sciences, April 1, 1993. (Chapter 5)

Zilinskas, Raymond, "Biological Warfare and the Third World," *Politics and the Life Sciences*, August 1990. (Chapter 2)

About the Authors

Randall Forsberg is director of the Institute for Defense and Disarmament Studies, in Cambridge, Massachusetts, which she founded in 1979. She started working in the field of disarmament at the Stockholm International Peace Research Institute (SIPRI) in Sweden in 1968. In the early 1980s she drafted the original proposal for a bilateral freeze on the testing, production, and deployment of nuclear weapons, and she helped found and lead the national Nuclear Weapons Freeze Campaign. A recipient of a five-year MacArthur Foundation Fellowship, she has been an innovator in efforts to demilitarize foreign policy, promote peace and democracy, and make deep cuts in military spending. Since 1990 she has been working on various aspects of a cooperative security system, including conventional arms reductions and multilateral peacekeeping. Her main focus at the Institute for Defense and Disarmament Studies today is a study of cooperative restraints on arms deployment, production, and trade, a joint project of centers in seven countries to explore ways to reduce standing armed forces, mothball defense industries, and reduce major arms exports. She is also working on a book on the link between the spread of democratic values and changing attitudes toward the use of force.

William Driscoll is a professional writer and editor and currently works as a project manager for ICF Incorporated, a consulting firm that prepares economic and regulatory analyses for the US Environmental Protection Agency. He participated in the nuclear disarmament and safe energy movements of the late 1970s and early 1980s, including campaigns that succeeded in stopping construction of the Seabrook II and Shoreham nuclear reactors. He holds degrees from Yale (B.A. in history, 1983) and Princeton (M.A. in public affairs from the Woodrow Wilson School, 1991).

Gregory Webb is editor of *The Arms Control Reporter*, published monthly by the Institute for Defense and Disarmament Studies. Before joining the *Reporter* staff in 1993, he was assistant editor of *Arms Control Today*, published by the Arms Control Association.

Jonathan Dean is adviser on international security issues to the Union of Concerned Scientists. As US diplomat working mainly on international security, European security, nuclear arms control, and international peacekeeping, he served as US Representative to the NATO-Warsaw Pact force reduction talks in Vienna (MBFR) between 1978 and 1981, having served as Deputy US Representative from the beginning of these talks in 1973. He also served as Deputy US Negotiator for the 1971 Four Power Berlin Agreement with the Soviet Union that ended three decades of dangerous East-West wrangling over Berlin.

Ambassador Dean began his foreign service work in 1950 in Bonn as liaison officer between the US High Commission and the newly-formed Federal German government. His subsequent assignments included posts in Washington, Prague, Elisabethville (Katanga), and Bonn.

Ambassador Dean has written extensively on national security policy, arms control, peacekeeping, German and East European issues, and European security problems. He is the author of *Watershed in Europe* (1987), *Meeting Gorbachev's Challenge* (1990), and *Ending Europe's Wars* (Twentieth Century Fund Press, 1994) on Europe's post–Cold War security problems.

Ambassador Dean is a graduate of the National War College and holds a Ph.D. in Political Science from George Washington University. He saw combat infantry service during World War II, from Normandy to the Elbe.

Index

About IDDS

Founded in 1979, the Institute for Defense and Disarmament Studies is a nonprofit center for research and education on ways to reduce the risk of war, minimize military spending, and promote the growth of democratic institutions.

Institute staff members study worldwide military forces and military and arms control policies. Since 1990, the Institute's research has focused on four areas of potential international cooperation on security policy: limiting the forces maintained for national defense to nonoffensive capabilities and strategies, aimed at defending territorial sovereignty and integrity with little or no threat of attack on other nations; replacing unilateral military intervention with multilateral peacemaking under UN or other nonpartisan auspices; ending the production and export of weapons that strengthen capabilities for international aggression or cross-border attack, except where such weapons are needed for multilateral peacemaking; and strengthening international institutions for nonviolent conflict resolution.

In 1992 the Institute organized a project on Global Restraints on Arms Deployment, Production, and Trade ("the International Fighter Study"), a collaborative effort with scholars from the main arms-producing and arms-importing nations to study ways to restrict weapons with long-range attack capability. The *Arms Production Dilemma,* the first of three planned volumes of the study, was published in 1994.

Other current studies at the Institute concern the implications of increased reliance on multilateral peacemaking for US forces and spending, and the political, ethical, and practical obstacles to an effective UN peacemaking capability. The Institute co-sponsors articles on security issues published in the *Boston Review*, distributing reprints to college teachers, public interest groups, journalists, members of government, diplomats, and independent analysts in the United States and other countries. In addition, the Institute offers bulk copies of the reprints free for use in classes and public programs.

The Institute's monthly journal, the *Arms Control Reporter*, published since 1982, is the leading international reference source on arms control negotiations.

IDDS Publications

Available from Commercial Publishers

Randall Forsberg, William Driscoll, Gregory Webb, and Jonathan Dean, *Nonproliferation Primer* (MIT Press: 1995), $14.95 paperback, plus shipping. Call 1-800-356-0343 to order.

Randall Forsberg, ed., *The Arms Production Dilemma: Contraction and Restraint in the World Combat Aircraft Industry* (MIT Press: 1994), 300 pages. $17.95 paperback (order no. FORFP), $39.95 hardcover (order no. FORFH), plus shipping. Call 1-800-356-0343 to order.

Tom Stefanick, *Strategic Antisubmarine Warfare and Naval Strategy* (Lexington Books: 1987), distributed by Simon & Schuster, 400 pages. $60 (order no. 00669140155), plus shipping. Call 1-800-223-2336 to order.

Neta Crawford, *World Weapon Database Vol. II: Soviet Military Aircraft* (Lexington Books: 1987), distributed by Simon & Schuster, 1,060 pages. $95 (order no. 0669148873), plus shipping. Call 1-800-223-2336 to order.

Barton Wright, *World Weapon Database Vol. I: Soviet Missiles* (Lexington Books: 1986), distributed by Simon & Schuster, 700 pages. $80 (order no. 066911786), plus shipping. Call 1-800-223-2336 to order.

Distributed by IDDS

Gregory Webb, ed., *Arms Control Reporter*, a monthly chronicle of arms control negotiations and agreements. Write for a price list.

Elmer Engstrom, *Analysis of US Army RDT&E Funding 1980–1995*, IDDS Budget Studies No. 1, forthcoming 1995. Free.

Jonathan Cohen and Andrew Peach, *IDDS Almanac 1994*, 140 pages. $30 plus shipping ($5 in North America, $15 elsewhere).

IDDS *Boston Review* Reprints (up to 100 copies free on request)
4. Forsberg, Arbatov, "Wasting Billions," *Boston Review* 19:2 (April-May 1994).
3. Otunnu and Cohen, Ahmad, Mehta, Henrikson, Forsberg, "The North-South Divide," *Boston Review* 18:3-4 (June-Aug 1993).
2. Forsberg, Van Evera, Alker, Dean, Kaysen, Landy, Miller, "Cooperative Security," *Boston Review* 17:6 (Nov-Dec 1992).
1. Forsberg, Bischak, Booth, and Anderson, "Defense Cuts and Cooperative Security," *Boston Review* 17:3-4 (May-June 1992).

For IDDS distribution, contact Jessie Saacke, IDDS, 675 Massachusetts Avenue., Cambridge MA 02139, USA. Tel: 617/354-4337, Fax: 617/354-1450